P9-CEJ-240

# SPECTACULAR STORIES FOR CURIOUS KIDS

Copyright ® 2021 Big Dreams Kids Books

Printed in the USA.

Book illustrations and cover design by Davor Ratkovic

# Contents

The Most Powerful Man in the World...
Defeated By Rabbits? ........................................................................9

Did Pablo Picasso steal the Mona Lisa? ...................................... 12

Parents Used To Be Able To Mail Their Kids ......................... 16

Helicopter Battles and Kidnappings in the
Smallest Country in the World? ..................................................... 18

The Creepy Curse of Tippecanoe ..................................................22

The Girl "Paul Revere" ....................................................................27

I Was Whale Food! ............................................................................29

The Most Difficult-To-Pronounce Town in the World??? ......32

Two Homeless Orphan Boys Who Were Friends, Both
Became...Governors? ........................................................................37

Selling Seashore Seashells ............................................................. 41

The Nobel Peace Prize is Named After the
Inventor of Dynamite ......................................................................43

A Ceasefire to Return a Dog to the Enemy ............................47

The Exploding Rat Strategy of WWII ................................49

A Cave With 5 Million Years of Unique Creatures ...............51

Did Both King Henry VIII and William the Conqueror's
Bodies Explode at Their Funerals??? ............................54

Night Writing in Wartime................................................57

Where Do Skeletons Dance and Mud Men Walk?.................61

You Can't Keep Our Pandas ..........................................65

Did An Ancient Curse Kill 22 Archaeologists?.....................67

Flying Sausages.............................................................70

A Spine Tingling Alabama Ghost Story...............................73

The Unicorn of a Nation................................................77

Lightning Is No Joke! ....................................................79

Was Alexander the Great Buried Alive?............................81

Over a Year Lost at Sea and Adrift for 6,700 Miles................84

Gaylord Perry's Moon Shot .............................................87

The Domino Effect .......................................................90

Were the Founding Fathers Really A Bunch of Old Guys?....93

Excuse Me, Have You Seen Any Vampires?..........................96

High Seas in High Heels?................................................99

That's the King's Pigeon Poop! ....................................103

Take This Mold Juice And Call Me In the Morning............105

This Masterpiece Stinks....................................................108

Just A Kid .......................................................................110

The Cobra Effect ...........................................................113

That Time A Best Selling Book Was Written
by a 9 Year Old................................................................116

Accidental Inventions.......................................................118

The 80's Called and They Want Their Phones Back............121

You Were Captured By Who? HOW?...............................123

It's Space Metal, Dude.....................................................127

A Bizarre Scientific Mystery.............................................129

Is It Breezy In Here? .......................................................131

You Do What?.................................................................133

Excuse Me? A Little Help Down Here?.............................135

That's No Ordinary Dog...................................................139

Take This Job and Shove It...............................................141

This Story Smells!............................................................143

Really? Again???............................................................145

Revenge of the Tooth Without a Body........................149

Did You Notice My Pineapple?...................................151

I Think I've Been Here Before....................................153

Death by Dancing.......................................................156

Robin Hood's Day Job.................................................159

The Shortest War in History Lasted for Less Than 45
Minutes....................................................................... 161

A Teddy Bear Origin Story.........................................165

Keep the Chocolate Train Going................................167

Don't Die Here............................................................169

Where Is His Mind? ....................................................171

The Royal Truck Mechanic.........................................173

Now Don't Move for 8 Hours..................................... 176

Land of the Flying Rhinos...........................................179

A World Without Ketchup?.........................................182

Don't Fear Falling From the Sky?...............................184

Typhoid Fever for You, and You, and You...................187

I got Shotgun!..................................................................... 191

The Man Who Saved Over 400 People from
Jumping Off a Bridge .........................................................195

200,000 Tons of Bombs, Quietly Lurking................................197

"Stop! Police Geese! Honk!"............................................... 200

How Could A Mom Fail 4 DNA Tests? ................................. 202

You'll Pry My Teacup From My Cold Dead Hands............. 205

What's for Dessert?............................................................. 207

Hey, We Can Fight Too! ..................................................... 209

Mummify Yourself...Alive ................................................. 212

The Mystery At Your Fingertips ......................................... 215

The Sandwich That Started A World War............................218

Can You Really Operate...on Yourself? .........................221

An Official Statement On Mermaids................................. 225

The First Person to Ride Down Niagara Falls in a
Barrel Was How Old?....................................................... 227

The Unhappy Drill Sergeant Who Became the World's
Happiest TV Painter......................................................... 230

The Man Sent to an Insane Asylum for Suggesting
Doctors Wash Their Hands.............................................. 233

The Boy Who Quit, 3 Feet Away From Gold.........................235

The $80 Champion ...................................................239

Do You Accept Checks?..............................................242

A Running Rebel ....................................................244

The First Two Cars in Ohio...Crashed Into Each Other......246

A 1 in 30 Million Rare Lobster Almost Eaten for Lunch....248

This Giant Might Be the World's Nicest, Most
Loveable Guy.........................................................251

The Greatest Fiasco in Swedish Naval History.................254

Get That Tower Outta Here!.......................................257

The Giant Hole That Sucks In Helicopters ....................259

Radioactive Spider Bites............................................262

You WON'T Pop Your Eye Out?.................................264

Weird Things About Abraham Lincoln's Assassination......267

The Doctor Who Ruled A Country...
Only To Lose His Head.............................................269

The Oldest Hotel in the World ...................................272

The Guy Who Had Hiccups...for 68 Years ...................274

Shakespeare's Curse...Couldn't Save His Head ...............277

# The Most Powerful Man in the World...Defeated By Rabbits?

When you think of Napoleon you think of the masterful leader, the military genius with many successful campaigns during the French Revolution. He dominated Europe in the 19th century and yet, he was no match for a horde of fluffy little bunnies.

Bunnies? Did you say bunnies? Yes, bunnies. Historians claim that Napoleon's worst defeat happened at Waterloo. But another disappointing defeat happened several years later, during an outdoor luncheon.

It was a pleasant summer day in 1807. Napoleon had just finished signing the Treaties of Tilsit, which ended the war with Russia. So he was feeling quite good about himself. Good enough to arrange a little get together with the biggest military names and indulge in a relaxing rabbit hunt. His Chief of Staff, Alexandre Berthier took it upon himself to organize the whole thing. He gathered approximately 3000 rabbits. They were held in cages along the fringes of a field. The plan was to release them once the hunt started.

But when released, the rabbits didn't run. They weren't scared in the slightest. On the contrary, they headed straight for Napoleon and the rest of the hunters. At first, everyone thought it was cute and funny.

Look at all those rabbits darting at us! But as the long-eared, fluffy ocean kept on hopping in their direction, it started to become less and less funny. Especially when the rabbits started climbing up Napoleon's trousers and jacket.

A crazy dance began. His men grabbed sticks, trying to shoo away the rabbits. Napoleon tried beating them back with his riding crop. Bullwhips snapped all around them. And yet the onslaught kept coming. There was no end to the bunnies. They just kept coming and coming.

Seeing he could not win this battle, Napoleon started to retreat to the safety of his carriage. One historian, David Chandler, had this to say about it. "With a finer understanding of Napoleonic strategy than most of his generals, the rabbit horde divided into two wings and poured around the flanks of the party and headed for the imperial coach." Some bunnies leaped into the carriage! As the coach drove away, they were finally able to lose the rabbits. Not even the man who had all of Europe in his grip was a match for these fuzzy little beasts.

So what happened? Why didn't they scurry away in fright? Berthier was to blame. Instead of making the effort to trap wild hares, he just went and bought the rabbits from local farmers. Tame rabbits. Rabbits who were used to humans being nearby and most importantly, providing food for them. So when the little bunnies saw all those people, they were like, "Woohoo! It's feeding time!"

The lesson here is if you are organizing a rabbit hunt for the world's great military leaders, be sure to feed the bunnies before the start of the hunt!

# Did Pablo Picasso steal
# the Mona Lisa?

In the early morning of August 21st, 1911, a man snuck out of the supply closet that he had hidden in overnight. He found one of the smallest paintings in the world famous Louvre museum in Paris, France and lifted the framed wooden canvas off the wall. He removed the painting from the frame and hid it under a large smock. Then he walked out into broad daylight where he boarded a train towards his home.

The thief had just stolen the Mona Lisa!

It may surprise you to know that no one even noticed the painting was gone for 28 hours. This is when a young artist who was hoping to paint a replica noticed it was missing. During this time in the Louvre's history, paintings were frequently moved around and photographed. The artist asked a guard to inquire when the painting would be returned. The guard searched for it and alerted the head of the museum. The painting was missing!

Why did it take them so long to even notice the Mona Lisa was gone? In 1911, the Mona Lisa was hardly a famous work of art. Created by Leonardo da Vinci in the very early 1500's, the painting was only really known by Renaissance art enthusiasts. But all of that was about to change.

A media frenzy began as word of the stolen painting spread. The French police closed all borders in case someone was trying to smuggle the painting out of the country. Newspapers all over the world reported on the stolen painting. Suddenly the Mona Lisa was famous! When the Louvre re-opened a week after the theft, people flocked in to see the bare spot where the painting had once hung.

There were many speculations about who had stolen the painting, but few leads. Some suspected American tycoon J.P. Morgan. The French were worried that wealthy Americans were going to buy up all of France's best artwork.

While police searched for leads, they were tipped off about other smaller artworks that had been stolen from the Louvre. This led them to the name Pablo Picasso. You may know him now as a very well known artist but at the time, Picasso was known as a bit of an art rebel. It came to the police's attention that Picasso was in possession of two stolen Iberian statues. The statues had been stolen by an acquaintance of Picasso and sold to him very cheaply.

Speculations began to fly and Picasso was brought in for questioning. On September 8 of 1911, he even went before a judge. While Picasso and his friend were being questioned they were both in hysterics, pleading with the court as to their innocence. The judge finally ruled that neither had anything to do with the Mona Lisa's disappearance and they were released four days later.

The trail went cold. For two years, nothing else was learned about the Mona Lisa. The painting was hiding in a trunk under the bed of the original thief.

But in November of 1913, the thief felt he had waited long enough. He reached out to an art dealer in Florence, Italy and told him he wanted to sell him the original Mona Lisa.

The thief was Italian born, Vincenzo Perugia. He stole the work of art because he felt that it belonged back in Italy, where Leonardo da Vinci had originally painted it.

The art dealer and Perugia worked out a deal. Perugia would sell the Mona Lisa to the Italian government for about $2 million, when really the painting was worth probably $20 million.

However, the art dealer was a good person and knew that this deal was not right. He met with Perugia to make sure that the painting was indeed the authentic Mona Lisa. It was! With the painting in his possession, he sent Perugia to a hotel to collect his payment. The police were notified and waited at the hotel to arrest Perugia.

Perugia went to jail and later to trial. He received a very light sentence of only 7 months. And because he had already served more than that while awaiting trial, he was immediately released. It is said that he had many Italian fans while he was in prison and would receive many cards and even cakes.

The Mona Lisa was returned to the Louvre in France where an estimated 100,000 people visited it on the first two days back in the museum. Today, because of this theft the Mona Lisa is one of the most well known paintings in the world. Nearly 20,000 people a day flock to the Louvre, just to get a glance at the woman with her coy smile.

# Parents Used To Be Able To Mail Their Kids

When the post office started offering deliveries of packages weighing over four pounds on January 1, 1913, there was at first, no postal regulation as to what you could send. So of course, people started testing these rules to see what they could get away with. They'd send bricks, live chickens along with eggs, and all sorts of weird stuff. But the weirdest thing ever sent through the post were probably children. Yup. Real, live, children. You may ask why on earth would parents send kids by mail? Well, because there were no rules that stated they couldn't! For some people, that is more than enough of a reason.

So how did this work? You take one baby, you slap a 15 cent stamp on its clothes, add about $50 for insurance (if the postman lost your baby, you'd want it back, right?), give the baby to the mailman, and voila! Easy peasy. This is exactly what an Ohio couple, the Beagues, did sending their infant son over to grandma's, who lived only a mile away.

There were about 17 recorded cases of people doing this between 1913 and 1915. Luckily, this wasn't a common practice. But as always, people wanted to cut corners and save a few pennies. It was actually cheaper to buy a stamp and use Railway Mail to send your kid as a piece of mail, than it was to buy your child a train ticket.

You'd think these people had gone crazy, giving their child off to a stranger, right? But keep in mind that this happened in rural areas, where almost everyone knew the mailman really well. They were friends, neighbors, and sometimes, as in the case of May Pierstorff, the mailman was even a close relative. So of course, May's parents had no problem sending little May to her grandparents' place via the Railway Mail train on a 73 mile journey. Her trip cost 53 cents for a stamp which was then dutifully placed on the six year old girl's coat.

The last kid package was delivered in August 1915, when Maud Smith who was only three was sent back home from her grandparents. The story eventually made the news, and the superintendent John Clark of the Cincinnati division of the Railway Mail Service finally put an end to it. After that, they would no longer allow kids to be classified as "harmless live animals".

# Helicopter Battles and Kidnappings in the Smallest Country in the World?

The year was 1965. This was the heyday of pirate radio. What the heck is that? A pirate radio station is one that broadcasts whatever they want...without a license. So they were basically rebels who did their thing beyond government control. This is the story of one such rebel.

But this story actually begins a little earlier in World War II. Great Britain had invested in the construction of lots of sea forts. The purpose of these forts was to protect the country from sneak attacks from Germany. Once the war was over, these forts were abandoned.

Paddy Roy Bates had spent a lot of time as a major in England's army. He was not a fan of state sponsored radio and had started his own station and really enjoyed it. The British government made it harder for him to broadcast, so he moved out to an abandoned outpost just beyond England's reach.

There was actually a pirate radio station already broadcasting from the old fort. But that didn't matter to Bates. He kicked them out somehow and took it for himself. And even though he had taken all of his radio equipment out there, he never broadcasted any radio from the fort. He decided that he was the leader of a new country. And that was much more exciting to him than being a radio broadcaster.

The fort was known as Fort Rough's Tower. It was located 7 miles off of England's eastern coast. Bates renamed the fort, Sealand. Then he presented it as a Christmas gift for his wife, Joan. Most people may not have been too excited about such a gift, much less actually moving out to a sea fort. But Joan was apparently a pretty good sport about the whole thing. Eventually she brought the couple's 14 year old son and 17 year old daughter and moved to what her husband was calling the smallest country in the world.

The Principality of Sealand as Bates was now calling it, was basically a large platform supported by two large round columns rising out of the sea from a sandbar, without any views of land. After a year of hearing about this family living on this ocean fort calling it a country, the British government had had enough. They were not willing to allow a new tiny independent country to spring up just off its coast. So the army was called in.

Here's where things start to get really exciting. Military boats and helicopters were sent on a mission to retake the little island for England. Explosives were dropped all around the platform making large explosions everywhere. Sailors from the army boat yelled at the family that they were next! "Prince" Michael, who was 15 at the time, fired several warning shots at the menacing helicopters and the army retreated.

Both Bates and his son, Michael were summoned with arrest warrants but a judge ruled that the British government had no authority to tell the family what to do or move them off the fort so they were released. As more years passed, over 50 people had moved out to the little micronation. They had electricity from a generator powered by the constant wind, with 10 rooms including a kitchen, a chapel and a living room. Much of this was in the hollow support columns holding up the entire structure.

Ten years after the Bates family had moved to Sealand, more high seas adventures would befall them. A former resident of the fort from Germany claimed that he was the true ruler of Sealand and while Paddy Roy Bates was away, he and his heavily armed mercenaries raided the fort with a helicopter and speedboats. Prince Michael was taken hostage and locked in a room for 4 days. Michael escaped and was able to get weapons the family had hidden at the fort. Along with his father's counterattack, the Bates family retook their country from the mercenaries without anyone getting injured. They kept the main instigator as a hostage and Germany sent their ambassador to negotiate his release.

Over the years Sealand has printed its own money and issued its own passports. The state flag of Sealand was even once placed on top of Mt. Everest. Michael Bates continued to live on the fort for many years but wanted his children to go to regular schools back in England. The "country" still exists today. Michael now lives in England with his large family but still claims

Sealand is it's own country even though it still isn't officially recognized.

The man behind this whole story, Paddy Roy Bates, is a real example of a rebel. He is known for saying, "I might die young or I might die old, but I will never die of boredom." By that standard he was certainly successful and led a most interesting and exciting life!

# The Creepy Curse of Tippecanoe

Curses are the intention to channel a supernatural power to cause harm or misfortune to another person. When something inexplicably bad happens (to you or someone else) and there's no rational belief to explain it, people can be eager to jump to the conclusion that someone put a curse on them. Here is the story of President William Henry Harrison, Shawnee leader Tecumseh, and the curse of Tippecanoe. The curse is that any U.S. president elected in a year ending with a "zero" would die while they were in office.

So what happened that caused this belief? The Battle of Tippecanoe took place in 1811. Harrison was the governor of the Indiana Territory, and he used some pretty unfair tactics while getting the Shawnee people to surrender possession of large parts of their land. Tecumseh thought Harrison was a scoundrel who was trying to cheat them, so he and his brother got other local tribes to join in and together, they attacked Harrison's army.

The US won the battle. Then in 1812, Harrison kept fueling this belief that he wasn't fond of indigenous tribes when he fought and won the Battle of the Thames against the British and the tribes who fought by their side. This loss led to more land being handed over to the US. The rage at this unfair treatment led to Tenskwatawa, Tecumseh's brother, putting a curse on all US presidents who were elected in years ending in a zero. That might seem a bit random, but Tenskwatawa was really mad.

Fast forward to 1840 when Harrison became the president of the United States. His slogan was "Tippecanoe and Tyler Too." Sounds a bit like rubbing salt on a wound, right? It was a cold and rainy day when Harrison gave his inaugural address on March 4, 1841, during which he caught a cold. At first it seemed like nothing. Just a cold, right? Not really. This simple cold turned into full blown pneumonia, and Harrison died only a month later, on April 4. This was the beginning of a series of presidential deaths for those who won the election at the start of a decade. It became known as Tecumseh's Curse, or The Curse of Tippecanoe.

Which other presidents fell victim to this supposed curse? Abraham Lincoln, for one. He was elected in 1860. Civil War erupted, and General Robert E. Lee surrendered to General Ulysses S. Grant. All seemed well. At least on the way to reparation. But then on April 14, 1865, John Wilkes Booth changed history forever when he shot Lincoln.

James Garfield became president in 1880. Just a few months after Garfield took office in 1881, Charles J. Guieteau was refused a diplomatic post by the president's administration, and thought this reason enough to shoot Garfield.

William McKinley was elected in 1900. This was his second term. He was shot on September 6, 1901, because Leon F. Czolgosz considered him an enemy of the people.

Warren Harding was elected in 1920. Funnily enough, he's actually considered one of the worst presidents of all time. And somehow, no one killed him. He suffered a stroke while visiting San Francisco.

Franklin Roosevelt was elected in 1932, 1936, 1940, and again in 1944. Maybe the curse skipped him over? Hardly. He died of cerebral hemorrhage in 1945. Some don't think he falls under the category of the curse, but others do because one of his terms (his third one) ended with a zero.

John F. Kennedy won the election in 1960, and became the youngest US president. Like other presidents, he had his ups and downs such as the Cuban Missile Crisis or the Bay of Pigs Invasion, but overall the people liked him. Everyone but Lee Harvey Oswald, who shot him on November 22, 1963.

So who broke the curse? It was Ronald Reagan. While Kennedy was the youngest elected president, Reagan was the oldest. He played a crucial role in the breakup of the Soviet Union. In 1981, John Hinckley Jr. shot him. But despite the curse, Reagan survived. As such, he's considered to be the one who broke the curse.

George W. Bush, who was elected in 2000, was also the survivor of two assassination attempts. Now with Joe Biden elected in 2020, we'll see if the curse has really been lifted.

# The Girl "Paul Revere"

You've no doubt heard of Paul Revere heroically riding at midnight to let everyone know that the British were coming. But have you heard of the 16 year old girl who was also riding at night? Sybil Ludington made her own heroic night ride, only she rode sidesaddle and rode much much further than Revere did.

Young Sybil lived with her family in Dutchess County, New York and was the oldest of twelve children. Her father was Colonel Henry Ludington who had fought in the French Indian War and was a highly respected military man. He was commander of the 7th Regiment that belonged to the Dutchess County Militia. This was a volunteer group of about 400 local men who had banded together to fight during the days of the Revolutionary War.

On April 25, 1777, British Commander General William Tryon landed with about 2000 men. They began to take over nearby Danbury, Connecticut, searching for the Continental Army supply storage and burning stores and houses. A messenger rider was sent to dispatch the message of the British attack to nearby towns. He arrived at the Ludington house around 9pm, too exhausted to go any further.

Colonel Ludington needed to gather his troops to prepare an attack. The problem was that most of his soldiers had already returned to their nearby homes to assist with spring planting. With the Colonel needing to plan his strategy, young Sybil dutifully took on the mission of rallying the troops and warning nearby neighbors.

Sixteen year old Sybil on top of Star (her horse), set out into the dark, rainy night. They rode through nearby farms and many dark desolate roads. She had a stick that she used to urge her horse forward and to tap on doors and windows.

"The British are burning Danbury. Muster at Ludington's at daybreak!" she was heard shouting on her all night ride. When she arrived home at sun-up that next morning, Sybil had covered over 40 miles. Nearly all of the 400 men had arrived at her father's farm and were prepared to march.

Although they were too late to save Danbury, the 7th Regiment was responsible for helping to drive the British troops back south towards the Long Island Sound where their ships were waiting.

Sybil was praised by her friends and neighbors as well as by the one and only, General George Washington. That was a great honor. But for the most part, few people know about the 16 year old's heroic ride. The Daughters of the American Revolution funded a statue of Sybil and Star in 1961 in Carmel, New York.

# I Was Whale Food!

Michael Packard is one of the best lobster divers in Cape Cod, but that didn't stop him from almost being a part of the ocean's food chain!

Lobster divers have to be tough to brave the cold and turbulent waters of the Atlantic Ocean. They literally swim down to the bottom of a sandy shelf on the ocean floor and pluck migrating lobsters off the bottom. Plenty of other sea creatures are inhabiting the same area as the lobsters, meaning it can be a good feeding ground for bigger fish.

Michael was swimming down about 10 feet from the bottom. He noticed several different schools of fish, sand lances and stripers swimming around him. Suddenly he felt a huge shove from behind and then everything went dark.

Michael wasn't unconscious. It was dark because he was inside the mouth of a giant creature. He could feel the mouth constricting around him! At first he thought he might have been swallowed by a great white shark, but then he realized there were no teeth. He had been swallowed by a humpback whale!

Michael began to struggle inside the whale's mouth. He could tell the whale didn't like it, so he tried to do it more. Michael thinks he was probably inside the whale's mouth for 30-40 seconds. Finally the whale came to the surface of the water, thrashed about and spit Michael out.

When Michael's crew member on his boat saw the fish submerge he thought it was a great white shark. Then he saw the whale spitting Michael out into the ocean. He hurried over to Michael and radioed for help. An ambulance met the boat and took Michael to the hospital. He was released later that day with some soft tissue damage, but no broken bones. Amazing!

So how likely is it that a person would get swallowed by a humpback whale? It's not very likely at all according to whale experts.

Humpback whales feed on the small schools of fish that can often be found around these sand bars. When the whales feed, their mouth billows out in front like a parachute which sometimes blocks their vision. The whale experts suspect that the whale that swallowed Michael was a medium sized young whale, who just happened to make a mistake when he was feeding that day.

Experts say that these whales have no teeth and their esophagus is actually too small to swallow anything large. However, as was the case with Micahel, a whale could wrap its mouth around a large object and spit it out. Whales without teeth, such as the humpback are not known to explore and cause damage with their mouths.

Is this the end of Michael's lobster diving? Nope! As soon as he is feeling better he hopes to be back in the water. Michael is no stranger to cheating death. In 2011, while in Costa Rica, Michael was in a small passenger plane that crashed in the jungle. Three people were killed instantly and the remaining five spent two nights in the jungle before they were found. So Michael has survived being a part of the food chain in both the ocean and the jungle. And you can swim confidently knowing that it is highly unlikely that you will ever be swallowed by a whale!

# The Most Difficult-To-Pronounce Town in the World???

Some countries require you to be a native, true-blooded citizen, in order to be able to pronounce the names of their towns. Wales is one of those countries. Nestled on the island of Great Britain as part of the United Kingdom, its history is long and vast. But there's a bit of a problem for tourists to this beautiful corner of the world. If you're not from there, it's a big, BIG challenge asking for directions because you won't be able to pronounce any place on the map!

I guess it's a lucky coincidence that the capital of Wales is Cardiff. Native or not, you'd know how to spell it and read it. But Cardiff is actually an exception to the general rule of naming Welsh cities and towns. They're usually so difficult to spell that not even Google has the right suggestion on how to correct your spelling. You're on your own on this one, I'm afraid.

So you've got places like Plwmp (pronounced as ploomp - you'd never guess, right?), or Ynysybwl (pronounced as [ənɪsə'bʊl]). Let's not forget Ysbyty Ystwyth, which is a small village in Wales that used to be under the rule of the Order of the Knights of the Hospital of St John of Jerusalem. The name is pronounced Esb'ti Esw'th, where Ysbyty means hospital.

As if these town tongue-twisters weren't enough, right? Now prepare to hear the name of the town with the most difficult pronunciation in the world.

Drum roll, please...

Llanfair-pwllgwyngyll-gogery-chwyrn-drobwll llan tysilio-gogo-goch!

How do you pronounce this? Ha! That's a good one. The only way to do this right is to get a Welsh person to pronounce it for you. But here, you can give it a go on your own:

/ɬanvairpʊɬɡʊiŋɨɬɡɔɡɛrɨxʊirn-drɔbʊɬlantisiliɔɡɔɡɔx/

What does the name mean? Brace yourself.

*Saint Mary's Church in the hollow of the white hazel near a rapid whirlpool and the Church of St. Tysilio of the red cave.* It's nice when people are this specific about a place, isn't it? At least you'd be able to find it easily, with that rapid whirlpool and red cave.

This town is actually quite lovely. You'll find it on an island just off of the northwest coast of Wales. It's a small town of only 3,000 people. This makes it just the 6th largest town on the island of Anglesey. Hey, that's not such a difficult name for the island, yay! Anyway, the town is very, very old. But it didn't receive it's super long name until the 1880's.

The town had previously been known as Llanfairpwll, which is hard enough. But according to legend, a tailor who lived there came up with a fun idea to really make map makers crazy. The idea was for the town to have the longest name in the world which would give its train station the longest sign in the country and attract visitors. It's really a sight to behold. All those letters just stretch on and on above the doors to the station.

The name boasts a staggering 58 characters, which makes it not only one of the most difficult names to pronounce, but also one of the longest names in the world. Of course, this means that the name, while lovely (if you can pronounce it, of course), is rather impractical. Just imagine having to write it down on an envelope. Yikes.

But the idea worked! Nearly 150 years later, this little island town of 3,000 people gets 200,000 visitors every year just because of its fun and crazily long name. Again, that's 200,000 tourists every year to a hard to find, tiny little island village!

It's obviously still a lot of fun for the town with the longest name in all of the United Kingdom. But they are actually no longer the longest town name in the world. Equally fun and silly people in New Zealand named their town, Tetaumatawhakatangihangakoau-aotamateaurehaeaturipukapihimaunga—horonukupo-kaiwhenuaakitanarahu.

And amazingly, at one point in history, Thailand's capital of Bangkok was called... Krung Thep Mahanakhon Amon Rattanakosin Mahinthara Ayuthaya Mahadilok Phop Noppharat Ratchathani Burirom Udomratchaniwet Mahasathan Amon Piman Awatan Sathit Sakkathattiya Witsanukam Prasit.

Oh boy. This story might be going off the rails. Back to Llanfairpwllgwyngyllgogerychwyrndrobwll-llantysiliogogogoch. Sometimes people have really big ideas. And sometimes that results in towns having really, REALLY big names!

# Two Homeless Orphan Boys Who Were Friends, Both Became... Governors?

Living in the streets of 1880 New York City was no walk in the park, especially for orphans. They had to resort to many things in order to feed themselves, like begging or shining shoes. On top of being hungry and cold, they also had to avoid angry, usually drunk adults who wouldn't refrain from beating them. Something had to change.

For those kids who wanted a fresh new start, one was provided in Iowa. They would travel by train for several days, from New York all the way to the rural Midwest. Scared but also hopeful, kids huddled next to one another, yearning for a better tomorrow with families where they would be adopted and put to field or farm work.

All this was way before there was any kind of protection for kids without parents. There was no social welfare. There was no foster care. Kids were left to fend for themselves. Help came in the guise of the orphan train movement. This movement was organized by reformers who wanted to protect all these poor, homeless, orphaned kids and provide them with a chance for a better future.

Between the years of 1854 and 1929, as many as 200,000-250,000 children were transported west on these trains. Can you imagine? Many had happy lives when they were adopted out West. Of course, many were not as lucky and lived as servants working all day on farms in return for food and shelter.

The man responsible for all this was named Charles Loring Brace. Times were hard and many people ended up on the streets, unable to take care of their kids. Some kids resorted to shining shoes and selling newspapers, but others turned to vagrancy and petty theft. It was obvious that the streets of the city were no place for children. Brace didn't want to throw these kids into prison with adults. The solution? Trains.

He said that "the best of all Asylums for the outcast child is the *farmer's home*." Farmers needed all the help they could get, and had lots of food and space to spare so it was a great combination. The children would be taken out west with a chaperone, then they'd be brought to large gatherings where potential parents might take a kid home with them. Agreements were signed that the children would be well taken care of.

There are thousands and thousands of amazing life stories of orphans who rode these trains from homelessness to their new destiny. One of the most compelling involves two boys who sat next to each other on one of these trains and became friends.

The year was 1859 and two tough kids used to living on the streets happened to be seated next to each other on one particular train with 27 kids on it. One was John Brady who was 11. John was so tough he already had a tattoo! The letters JB had been tattooed on his elbow. Ouch! John's mother tragically died when he was just a baby. And his cruel father beat him. He ran away at just 8 years old to live on the streets.

He sang old Irish songs on street corners, stole lead out of chimneys and sold it, and got money to survive any way that he could.

Sitting next to John on the train was Andrew Burke, an equally tough street urchin who had been an orphan since he was 4 years old. The two boys formed a deep and lasting friendship over the 7 day journey from New York to Indiana.

John was adopted by a state senator who thought he was the most unpromising kid on the train and was curious what he could do with such a specimen. Andrew was adopted by a farm family and in his teens became a drummer boy in the Civil War. Meanwhile, John had become a top student at his school. He didn't even get into too much trouble the time he knocked out a bully with one of his fists he had grown up using.

John grew up to be a preacher, moved to Alaska, became a judge, and over a number of years became governor of the entire state. His old friend Andrew had moved to North Dakota with $65 in his pocket. 10 years later, he was in charge of that entire state as it's governor.

59 years after these two unlikely future leaders met on that fateful day on an orphan train in 1859, they died exactly one month apart. These two lifelong

friends rose to great heights in life despite their tough beginnings. This story proves that no matter how many disadvantages we have or obstacles in our path, success is always possible.

# Selling Seashore Seashells

We all love tongue twisters, whether we're young or old. Can you can a can as a canner can can a can? Betty bought butter but the butter was bitter, so Betty bought better butter to make the bitter butter better. She sells seashells by the seashore. Try saying that fast. Did you know that last tongue twister, the one about seashells, was actually based on a real person?

Her name was Mary Anning, and what she was selling wasn't seashells but dinosaur fossils. She was born in 1799 and when she was only 12, she unearthed an ichthyosaurus skeleton on England's Dorset Beach. Not only was it 200 million years old, but the Geological Society in London recognized it as the first skeleton of its kind!

Mary Anning loved what she did, and it showed, so she eventually became the greatest fossilist of her time. She continued looking for other fossils, and was also important in figuring out that coprolites, which were called bezoar stones back then, were just fossilized doody.

But this love for fossils didn't start with her. It was her father who was an avid collector, and Mary, her brother, and her father, would wander around the cliffs carefully looking for specimens. Her father was the one who taught her how to identify the bones and how to collect them properly so that they wouldn't get damaged. Mary's father died in 1810, and without him to take care of the family, they were dependent on charity.

This was when Mary stepped up and opened up a family fossil business in 1820. While it was true that she lacked formal schooling, she was incredible in reading, writing, drawing and reconstructing a whole dinosaur skeleton. People flocked to her shop, buying her drawings and fossils. This included museum representatives, scientists, tourists, and even noblemen who wanted a fancy dinosaur fossil for their collection.

Despite everything, Mary and her family still had financial woes. Plus, because she was uneducated and had the audacity to be a woman, Oxford-based scientists would steal her work (writings and drawings) and publish them as their own. The idea that a poor spinster would dig up something so monumental sounded ridiculous. She wasn't taken seriously at all until French anatomist Georges Cuvier officially declared that the plesiosaur specimen she found was the real deal.

After her death at the young age of only 47, she was placed as the third most important British woman scientist, and her importance is still growing.

But a question remains. Did Mary Anning really sell seashells by the seashore? She most certainly did. The best seashells you could ever imagine.

# The Nobel Peace Prize is Named After the Inventor of Dynamite

In today's world, it seems we need peace more than anything else. And the Nobel Peace Prize rewards exactly that...extraordinary efforts in the field of creating peace in the world. So naturally, you'd think it was named after a Buddhist monk or something, right?

Wrong. It was actually named after the inventor of dynamite. Yes, you read that right. Dynamite is pretty much the exact opposite of peace. Still, in Alfred Nobel's defense, his discovery was caused by a tragedy that struck close to home. His younger brother's death in 1864 was the result of an uncontrolled explosion.

A native of Sweden, Alfred worked at his father's arms factory in his late twenties. The factory was employed in making military equipment for the Crimean War. This of course, meant that he knew a lot about chemistry and he also worked with all sorts of explosives. In 1864, a big factory explosion happened, and it took the lives of five people. This included the life of Alfred's younger brother. Understandably Alfred was deeply saddened, but eventually, he found light at the end of this dark tunnel. How?

He decided to develop a much safer explosive, one that could be controlled more easily. Dynamite is a concoction of something called nitroglycerin and an absorbent substance. Back in 1867 when he patented it, not many people knew of nitroglycerin. Today, it is widely understood that nitroglycerin is what makes things go "ka-boom".

Alfred thought that after his own death, people would remember him fondly for coming up with dynamite. After all, its safe handling has been extensively used in many aspects of everyday life. Unfortunately, a funny thing happened which assured him this wouldn't be the case.

That funny thing took place in 1888, when Alfred's other brother died in France. An obituary was published, only someone at a French newspaper mistakenly thought that it was Alfred who died, and not his brother. They went on to criticize him, even after death, for inventing dynamite.

Alfred was understandably upset. Shocked, even. He thought he'd be remembered as someone who made the world a better place. He became determined to correct this. He took out a chunk of his wealth and set it aside for a special assignment. That assignment was to establish prizes for outstanding men and women who made a significant and worthy contribution to the worlds of physics, medicine, literature, chemistry and world peace. He named it the Nobel Prize.

After his death in 1896, he left around $250 million dollars for the funding of future Nobel Prizes.

Now when we hear the name Nobel, we think of the good dude who decided to reward and inspire all those who make the world a better place, instead of the guy who invented dynamite.

# A Ceasefire to Return a
# Dog to the Enemy

It's October 4th, 1777 and a heavy fog has fallen over the suburbs of Philadelphia. You take advantage of the fog and lead your colonial troops to attack the unsuspecting British army. However, it doesn't go as planned and in the darkness your troops mostly end up accidentally firing at each other. Your great plan has gone awry when suddenly one of your soldiers brings you a little dog. The collar on the dog reads 'William Howe,' the General of the opposing British troops. What do you do?

If you're George Washington, an avid dog lover, you want to make sure the enemy General gets back his pet. And that's just what he did!

During the Revolutionary War, General George Washington was leading his troops into what he thought was clearly going to be a victorious battle. Using the fog as cover, his troops surrounded the British army and began firing. However, the fog made it difficult to see and the troops ended up firing at each other. The British General doesn't even realize they are under attack. He investigates what he thinks is just a few rebels firing their guns when his small terrier dog gets separated from him in the fog.

Washington's troops find the dog and bring him to Washington. They were probably thinking that this would be a delightful way to get back at the British General for their recent losses. If nothing else, holding the dog as ransom would surely bring down the morale of General Howe.

But General Washington was an honest man and a dog lover. What he did surprised his troops. He ordered a ceasefire. He wanted to be sure that the little dog made his way safely back to his rightful owner. And while they were waiting to return the dog, Washington made sure the dog had the best care. He personally brushed the mud from his fur, fed and watered him.

A messenger delivered the dog back to British troops with a note pinned to his collar that read. "General Washington's compliments to General Howe, does himself the pleasure to return him a Dog, which accidentally fell into his hands, and by the inscription on the Collar appears to belong to General Howe."

Some historians believe that perhaps General Washington was using this as a military tactic as a way to scout and gain some knowledge of the British camp. Other historians firmly believe that Washington was just a good guy who liked dogs and wanted to do the right thing. Either way, I'm sure General Howe and the little terrier were very appreciative to Washington for their reunion!

# The Exploding Rat
# Strategy of WWII

Have you ever heard the expression, "All is fair in love and war?" It basically means that when you're trying to win a war, anything goes. This has made for some very interesting wartime strategies over the course of human history.

One that is as fascinating as it is bizarre is the British attempt to use exploding rats to blow up German war factories. Wow. Just how would someone go about this? Can rats be trained for deadly sneak attacks? Well, it was the early 1940's and World War II was raging across Europe.

The plan went like this. British scientists filled dead rats with explosives to be little mini bombs, but disguised as rats. Then they would have secret agents sneak into the German weapon factories, and leave the rats lying around the factory boiler rooms.

The idea was that a German factory worker would see the rat and throw it in the furnace which would create a big explosion and stop them from making weapons for the German army. A lot has to go right for that to work. But was it worth a try? It turns out that the answer is yes. The plan worked! But not in the way the rat stuffing scientists had thought.

The very first shipment of rat bombs fell into enemy hands. Imagine being a German soldier, opening a box that was intended for British secret agents and seeing 100 dead rats. What must he have thought when he first saw that? Can you imagine?

So there wasn't a single known instance of a rat bomb blowing up a German factory. But when the Germans found them and discovered that they were actually disguised bombs, they had no idea that they had the first and only real batch of them. They thought there were thousands of them already all over their factories.

They spent hundreds of hours looking for rat bombs everywhere after this. This made the simple strategy a great success. Even more than if they had managed to blow up a factory furnace. If I found a box filled with stuffed rat bombs that was sent to my house, I'd be pretty nervous too!

# A Cave With 5 Million Years of
# Unique Creatures

Imagine a place that has been closed up from the rest of the world for 5 million years. Yes, 5 million...not 5 thousand. Take into account that humans have only been around for 300,000 to 400,000 years. Now back to this closed up place. There is no entrance, hence no exit either. All the air inside has been long substituted by toxic gases. And who knows what kind of monsters have been brewing inside that toxic soup.

Now imagine opening that place up. Scary! Who'd want to do that? Well, Dr. Cristian Lascu wanted to, for one. He opened one exact such place, now known as the Movile Cave in Romania.

The level of oxygen is much lower there than above ground. There is only 7 to 10% of it in the cave, while we have up to 21% of it in the air around us. As for carbon dioxide, get ready to be stumped. There is roughly one hundred times more of it in the cave than there is outside. Around us there is only 0.04%, while the cave boasts a whopping 2 to 3.5%! And that's not all to this poisonous concoction. There's also methane, hydrogen sulfide, and ammonia. Can you imagine that gross smell?

You'd think no animal could ever survive here, right? Wrong. There are as many as 69 species living in this noxious hodgepodge, such as spiders, scorpions, leeches, woodlice, one snail (who's a late comer, he arrived about 2 million years late to the party) and one centipede, who seems to be the king of the cave. That's actually what the scientists named him, *Cryptops speleorex*. He's the smallest king you've ever heard of at just 2 inches long, but he rules with a deadly bite.

Just entering the cave could be deadly, as the explorers climb down a small passageway, then weave through winding tunnels until they reach a cavern with a lake. If they want to explore the rest of the cave, they have to do it underwater and in pitch darkness. Sounds a tad unnerving, doesn't it?

The awesome part is that 34 species of the invertebrates found in this cave can't be found anywhere else in the world. They're totally unique to this deadly and toxic habitat. Because the cave is dark, all of them are blind with colorless bodies. How do they move without knowing where to go? They've got long antennas and even longer limbs. I'd hate to see any of those creepy crawlies.

But everything in this cave has an order. It's an entire ecosystem of its own. The bacteria inside the cave convert toxic gases into food via a clever process called chemosynthesis. It's something like photosynthesis in plants. Then, worms and shrimp feed on the bacteria while scorpions and spiders feed on the worms. The cycle is very well arranged and it's been functioning for 5 million years without human interference. Interestingly enough, such untouched ecosystems can usually be found only under water, deep inside oceans. This cave is special because it is an isolated ecosystem on land.

About as many people have been in this cave as there have who have flown to the moon. Only about 100 scientists over the last 30 years have been in there since the cave was first discovered. How many other strange mysteries must there still be lurking beneath our feet?

# Did Both King Henry VIII and William the Conqueror's Bodies Explode at Their Funerals???

Gross! That's the last thing that should ever happen at a funeral. But times were different many centuries ago. Basically, the world has always been pretty weird. But could it have been this weird? I mean...exploding bodies of kings at their own funerals? Let's dive in.

First of all, King Henry the 8th and William the Conqueror are two of history's not-so-great dudes. There were lots of executions, killing, and of course... conquering. And nobody likes to be conquered. It just isn't nice.

William the Conqueror died in 1087 after being the King of England for just over 20 years. Henry the 8th died almost 500 years later in 1547 after being the King of England for 37 years.

These were clearly two of history's heavyweights. And by that I mean very important people. But let's get to their funerals. Wait, we should probably start with how they died. William the Conqueror as you might guess died in battle. He spent a lot of time on the battlefield. It was one of his favorite places.

He didn't die there though. He was wounded badly and died later. The room where his body was laid after his death was looted pretty much immediately.

The thieves took everything but the king's naked body. It was left lying on the floor. It took awhile for monks to come and get the body ready for burial.

By the time William the Conqueror was finally ready to be buried, his bloated body would not fit in the stone coffin that had been made for him. This is where this story gets a bit gross. They tried to force the body into the coffin anyway and the body burst open. Is that another word for explode? Sort of. And I'm sorry. I'm really not trying to gross you out. But that's what happened according to people who wrote about it. The funny part is that the smell was so disgusting and horrible that no amount of incense helped at all. So they rushed through the rest of the funeral as fast as they could.

King Henry on the other hand, died at his palace from natural causes, not from battlefield wounds. His death wasn't announced for 3 days and then there were 10 days of religious ceremonies after that. That's a long time for a dead body to lay around. You probably know where this is going. After a person has died, the body starts to decompose which lets out gases. Those gases have to go somewhere.

Finally, it's time to bury the guy. But first, a 2 day procession to the church where other royals were buried had to happen. This procession was a huge spectacle. It stretched four miles long with horses, soldiers, and mourners of the king. There were more than 1,000 people in the procession and all the country came out to watch it pass by. People were actually paid to show up and pray as the procession moved past.

Henry's coffin was carried by a giant chariot that had to be pulled by 8 horses. It was quite the show. The funeral procession stopped overnight at a monastery where the "explosion" finally took place. Apparently King Henry's body had endured all it could. King Henry was a very large man and like William the Conqueror, had to be stuffed into his coffin. At this point, he's been in there for over 2 weeks.

According to legend, sometime during the night the coffin exploded and the dogs licked up remains of the king off the ground. Yikes! Did these exploding body stories of kings really happen? There's probably *some* truth to these stories. After all, the bodies weren't refrigerated in any way. But it's also quite likely that they were embellished to discredit the two kings. In either case, it sure makes for an interesting but gross story.

# Night Writing in Wartime

Braille is the alphabet for the blind. It's a system for reading and writing that is based on the tactical sense of touch. But did you know that this raised-dot writing and reading system wasn't initially intended for this purpose, but was actually meant to help French soldiers read combat messages in the dark?

To someone who's not really familiar with it, Braille looks hard. And it is. Just like any other alphabet, you need to learn it first to be able to do it. Every letter of the alphabet has an equivalent symbol in raised dots. This includes punctuation marks as well. You read Braille by moving your hand or hands left to right over the dots. The index finger is the one doing the reading at an average speed of 70-100 words per minute.

Providing an alphabet for the blind has enriched their lives immensely because it has allowed them the opportunity to read anything from restaurant menus to financial statements from their bank, or contracts that need to be signed. Before Braille, several attempts were created to help the blind read. They weren't raised dots, but raised versions of actual letters. You can imagine how hard that would be to read with your index finger. The alphabet we know was devised to be read with the eyes, so it was a tedious process to feel it with your fingers. But once Braille appeared, it was an instant success.

So how was it invented in the first place? In the beginning, it wasn't called Braille at all. It was "night-writing". It all started somewhere in the early 1800s. Napoleon's army was engaged in battle (as it usually was) and messages needed to be dispersed. Reading them during the night was particularly hard. You'd have to do this by lamp light. But that wasn't safe because shining a light in the dead of night revealed your exact location to your enemy. Charles Barbier, a military veteran in Napoleon's army, saw far too many deaths that were the result of shining lamps to read messages.

So he came up with an idea to prevent this from happening. He devised a night-writing system with raised dots. Every letter or phonetic sound had an equivalent in this system. The only problem was that the fingertip couldn't feel all the dots with one touch.

A few years later, Louis Braille was born just outside of Paris. He knew the struggles of being blind because he lost his eyesight as a small boy during a tragic accident. When he was 3 years old, he stabbed himself in the eye with his father's awl (an awl is a tool for making holes in leather). The infection from the wound spread to both eyes causing him to lose sight in both. Still, he didn't let this hold him down. When he was just 11 years old, he discovered the night-writing code that was developed by his fellow countryman, Barbier. This excited and inspired him and he came up with an ingenious idea. He would modify it to suit the blind.

He first presented it when he was just 15 years old but would spend the rest of his life perfecting it. The end result was a masterpiece that the blind still use today. To honor him, it was named Braille. What he did was make the dots more compact so that now a fingertip could feel the whole unit which allowed for faster comprehension and quicker reading. Even today, the basics of his alphabet are the same as when he invented it. Some small modifications were introduced, but it's only in the form of contractions. Just like you would contract can not to can't, for example.

Braille died very young. He was only 43, and he didn't live to see his home country of France adopt Braille as the official communication system for the blind. But his legacy lives on, allowing the sightless to "see" through their fingers.

# Where Do Skeletons Dance and Mud Men Walk?

One of the most fascinating and interesting places in the world has got to be the island of New Guinea. It is located just north of Australia in the south Pacific. It is the world's second largest island, only smaller than Greenland. What makes this island so incredible and unique is how many different cultures exist there. You can find over 850 languages spoken on this island. That is truly incredible.

There are also over 600 different tribes with their own cultures. These tribes are so fascinating because for hundreds of years, they were mostly cut off from the outside world. They were even mostly cut off from each other. This allowed for their traditions and practices to vary greatly.

Only in the last 100 years have we really been learning about all of these distinct cultures. There are three that really stand out to me. These include the Huli Wigmen, the Asaro Mudmen, and the Chimbu skeleton dancers.

Let's start with the Asaro Mudmen. Their ceremonial dance is otherworldly. It can be quite spooky. According to the legend that these people have passed down through the generations, they were attacked by a bigger tribe and forced to run away and hide in the Asaro river.

They waited until it started to get dark and rose from the banks of the river covered in mud and clay. This made for a startling scene and nearly scared the other tribe to death! The larger tribe ran away as fast as they could thinking they were seeing ghosts.

Their ceremonial clay masks, made from the clay of the Asaro river, don't crack when they dry. They can weigh more than 20 pounds and are quite scary looking. The Asaro people also wear bamboo stalks on their fingers when they reenact this legend which makes them look like they have giant claws that they click together. But underneath these costumes, they are just normal people. They don't live in these costumes, they are only for ceremonial dances.

The Huli Wigmen are another fascinating cultural story. The Huli men are well known for wearing great headdresses of real hair on their heads. In Huli culture, boys live with their moms until they are around 7 or 8 years old. Then they live with their dads and learn hunting and building skills. When these boys are around 14 years old, they go to wig school where they may live for up to 10 years.

Wig school is a coming of age, rite of passage. They grow their own hair out for a year and a half and then cut it and give it to the wig specialist who makes their ceremonial wig. While growing their hair, they sleep in a special position. They prop themselves up on an elbow and use a log for a pillow to grow their hair faster. It doesn't sound too comfortable does it? Many Huli men wear their wigs every day and have special wigs for their traditional ceremonies.

The final tribe I will highlight here is the Chimbu tribe. Like the Asaro Mudmen, they have a special way of decorating their bodies to strike fear in the hearts of their enemies.

These people live very remotely and are difficult to get to. They live in mountain valleys near the highest mountain in New Guinea, Mt. Wilhelm. The land is difficult. The Chimbu have a history of tending to herds of pigs they raise for food.

They are known for 'sing sing', a big festival where they perform their traditional dance. They spend many hours painting their bodies black with white bones to resemble skeletons. According to legend, the Chimbu ancestors were scared of a ghost that lived high up on the mountain.

When they hunted and went into the forest to gather food, they were scared of this ghost and thought that it would come down from its mountain cave and eat them. So they dressed up as the dead and shuffled like zombies to scare and trick the ghost. This also served to really scare their enemies in battle. Today, the Chimbu people are no longer scared of ghosts but perform the dance as a celebration of their history and tradition.

If you were born somewhere else in your own country, your life would probably be very different. But what if you were born in New Guinea? What interesting ways might you be living today? People live in all kinds of different ways all over the world. But some of the most fascinating traditions can be found on this Pacific island among the great cultures of the people living there.

# You Can't Keep Our Pandas

If you've been to a zoo, you've probably seen those adorable black and white furballs, the panda bears. Pandas are native to only one country. China. This means that China has absolute monopoly over them, and can use these bears for political influence. President Mao even used to give pandas as presents to his political allies. That practice stopped in 1984 when pandas made the endangered species list. Every panda you see in any country other than China is basically on loan, and after a designated time has passed, the contract is either prolonged or the panda goes back to China (even if it was born in another country).

So what's up with this rent-a-panda strategy? It's all politics. China started renting out pandas to foreign zoos, for a staggering price of $50,000 per month. Per month! This brought a lot of money into the country of China and eventually this turned into long-term loans.

Not surprisingly, China started using the pandas also as a reward or punishment. Many pandas found new (temporary) homes in France and Australia, simply because these countries focused on their nuclear industries, and China wanted to be onboard. Another example involves the country of Norway. China used to import salmon from Norway. But then the Nobel Peace Prize committee (a Norwegian committee) awarded a Nobel Prize to Liu Xiaobo, a man who was known for speaking out against the Chinese government. The Chinese said nothing. They just took their salmon business to Scotland. This is why Edinburgh, Scotland has its very own panda now.

In 2012, China promised Malaysia a pair of pandas. They signed the contract, and the cute pair was to arrive at the Kuala Lumpur Zoo in April 2014. Only, they didn't. April came and went. No pandas. Why? The Chinese were upset with the Malaysians because they didn't think the Malaysians were doing a very good job of handling the missing Malaysian Airlines flight MH 370. So the Chinese made them wait for the pandas for a whole month. Talk about sulking.

So what is the current cost of panda rental? The pandas need to be rented in pairs. Each panda is leased for $1million per year. Most contracts are for 10 years so you are looking at an investment of about $20 million for the two pandas. And if a baby is born while it is away on lease? The Chinese government charges an additional $500,000 baby tax! Better start saving your birthday money.

# Did An Ancient Curse Kill 22 Archaeologists?

Life as an archaeologist is hard work. Even the movies make it out that way! If Indiana Jones doesn't run really fast he gets crushed by rolling boulders and shot by poison tipped arrows, and on and on. While archaeology isn't THAT dangerous, it might be that those Indiana Jones movies weren't as far off as some have thought.

Tutankahamun's tomb was discovered nearly 100 years ago in 1922...completely intact. Tomb raiders had failed to find it as they had done with most ancient burial chambers. This made the discovery a remarkable one. The 3,000 year old tomb was filled with artifacts and set the world abuzz with excitement.

King Tut, as he is commonly referred to, died when he was just 18 years old. He actually became king when he was only 8 or 9. Holy cow! Can you imagine?

When the tomb was discovered by Howard Carter and Lord Carnarvon after years of searching, they would have been the first two people to step inside it in 3,000 years. Could they have unleashed an ancient curse?

Many believe in the so-called Mummy's Curse or Curse of the Pharaohs. According to legend, inscribed on many tombs in the ancient language of hieroglyph-ics is the following quote.

*'Death will slay with his wings whoever disturbs the pharaoh's peace.'*

Spooky! Is it true? One famous Egyptologist tells a story of Howard Carter after he first opened the tomb. He sent a messenger to his house. As the messenger approached Carter's home, he heard the sound of a "faint, almost human cry." When the messenger got up to the house he could see a birdcage inside with a King Cobra snake inside it. The snake had eaten the canary that lived in the cage. What's interesting is that on the day that Carter entered the tomb, the symbol of the pharaoh had broken into *his* house. The cobra was on all of the pharaoh's masks and was the symbol of the pharaoh striking his enemies. News of a curse spread quickly.

Lord Carnarvon was the first to die. He had fi-nanced the mission and was there when the tomb was discovered. He had a mosquito bite on his cheek that he cut during a shave. The wound got infected and he died 2 weeks later, 5 months after entering the tomb. News reports claimed that at the exact time of his death, the lights in Cairo mysteriously flickered.

Within 7 years, a total of 22 people who had en-tered King Tut's tomb died under mysterious and strange circumstances. Howard Carter wasn't one of them, however. He lived a long life. But he had giv-en a gift from the tomb to one of his friends. It was a mummified hand wearing a bracelet. On the bracelet was written, *"Cursed be he who moves my body. To him shall come fire, water, and pestilence."* Gee, thanks! The friend's house burned down soon after getting the hand. And when he rebuilt the house, it flooded. Got goosebumps yet?

If you research this yourself, you'll mostly read about how curses aren't real, including this one. But then again, I wouldn't blame you if you decided to be *really* careful about entering ancient tombs...

# Flying Sausages

Jokes about German sausage are the wurst! That was at least, what the Germans thought during WWI, when their government banned sausage-making for the simple reason that sausage casings were essential to their war efforts. And I do mean essential.

You're probably wondering why. Well, let me break it down for you. Sausage casings were (and still are, actually) made mostly of cow intestines because they're simply the largest, most readily available. The casings are what hold sausage together. During the war, they were neatly taken out of cows, emptied, washed, stretched, dried, then sewn together to create this amazingly huge balloon. It needed to be airtight, because it would be filled with hydrogen to help it fly high in the sky. Sausage casings were used in the creation of zeppelins, the huge airships that the Germans used to drop bombs.

WWI was fought on all levels, on the ground, below the ground, underwater, and in the skies. You name it. While contemporary combat doesn't use zeppelins anymore, they were quite a sight to behold back in the day. Although they weren't very precise, they were still massive and frightening. And, because of their humongous size, they eventually found their use in supply and soldier transport, in spotting submarines, and basically acting out the role of a hovering bodyguard to those below. Pretty neat, huh?

First, the zeppelins were made of rubber, but that didn't prove to be a good option. Then, someone came up with an ingenious idea. *Why don't we make them from guts?*

Once cow intestines were cleaned and dried properly, they created these super airtight seals. Not even rubber could be sealed like that. And it was exactly that seal that was crucial in making the zeppelin fly. You see, hydrogen is the lightest element and it could escape through even the tiniest hole. The zeppelins needed to be airtight for these airships to actually fly.

Imagine the size of those zeppelins. Colossal, right? Definitely. It took about 250,000 cow intestines for just one zeppelin. That's a lot of cow intestines! You see now why the Germans could not make sausage. The government even supervised butchers and public kitchens to make sure that no one was keeping any sausage casing for themselves. Doing that could land you some serious prison time.

So while the Germans yearned for their sausages, the British were biting their nails, trying to come up with a way to bring down those hydrogen monsters in the skies. Eventually they thought of a way. Shoot it with regular bullets first, then with bullets lined with phosphorus, so when those bullets came into contact with the hydrogen inside...kaboom. Zeppelin gone.

In the end, two very important questions remain.

Could the Germans make sausages without the casings? Sure. It would be just ground meat, which you could make into patties or something.

Would the Germans make such "sausages" without the casings? Surely not.

# A Spine Tingling Alabama Ghost Story

"....On a cold, dark, rainy night.....so bitterly cold, damp, and dark.....when even street lights won't burn, and the striking of a match refuses to yield the tiniest flame....on nights like this, Huggin' Molly comes out of her lair and roams the streets of Abbeville to see whom she can find."

Thus begins a ghost story that's been told for over 100 years...the story of Huggin' Molly. The origins are a little unclear, and the stories vary in detail, but all across Abbeville, Alabama, citizens shiver just a little when the local ghost, Huggin' Molly comes up in conversation.

Huggin' Molly is said to be 7 feet tall, and a very round woman dressed in a trailing long black dress. She hides in the shadows after dark, waiting for her victims to pass by so she can grab them, fiercely hugging them and often screaming in their ear.

The origin of the ghost varies a little within the citizens in the town. Some say that Huggin' Molly is the ghost of a woman who lost her young child tragically. She haunts the streets of Abbeville after dark, searching for her lost child. When she comes across an unattended child, she grabs and hugs it, screaming when she realizes the child is not her own.

Another tale is that the original Huggin' Molly may have been a professor at the former Southeast Alabama Agriculture School. The very tall professor worried about the safety of students out after dark, so he would dress in a large black cape and scare students who were out so they would hurry back to their dorms.

Others believe it is just a story passed down and told when parents didn't want their children out late. Parents would warn their children that if they didn't get home in time, Huggin' Molly was sure to get them in the dark.

Several residents of Abbeville have shared and passed on tales of their encounters with Huggin' Molly. One such story that has been passed along is from Mack Gregory, born in 1901. When Mack was a teenager, he was a grocery delivery boy. One day, he was just finishing up his deliveries when it began to get dark. In those days there were no street lamps on the side streets so it was very dark.

Mack heard footsteps, as if someone was following him. He quickened his pace and found the footsteps quickening also! When he took a quick glance he could just make out a very tall, black robed being, about 30 feet behind him. Afraid to run for fear the figure could easily get him, Mack kept a brisk pace all the way back to his house. He was able to make it safely into the security of his well-lit home. And once he was inside, the dark figure slowly continued down the sidewalk past his house. Phew! Mack made sure that he never again failed to deliver the groceries before the sun had set and darkness fell on the streets of Abbeville.

Though there are several versions of the tale of Huggin' Molly, it's for sure made Abbeville's young kids and teenagers cautious when they are out late at night. And the ghost has brought some bone-chilling fun to the residents of the town. There is even a restaurant in town now, called Huggin' Molly's. They serve up specials like "sandwitches" and "Molly Fingers." Perhaps you'd like to plan a trip to Abbeville to see what all the fuss is about. Just be sure to make it inside before dark!

# The Unicorn of a Nation

Many countries have chosen a national animal. Some are very famous, such as Australia and its kangaroo, India and its Bengal tiger, New Zealand and its kiwi bird, the United States and its bald eagle. Some countries even went so far as to choose a mythical animal, like the Scots did, opting for the unicorn (yes, the famous horse with a horn in the middle of its forehead).

In their defense, the Scots have always been famous for their love of myths and legends. Their history boasts stories of witches, all sorts of water monsters (Loch Ness anyone?), magic, ghosts, and the like. It's no wonder then that they chose the magical unicorn as their national animal.

Today we associate unicorns with sparkly, glittery horses, rainbow-colored tails and manes, and pink bodies. The girly version. The Scots however, see it as the epitome of bravery, a majestic horse boasting dominance, authority and courage. It just happens to have a big horn in the middle of its forehead. Their version of the unicorn is always pristine white, with a lush mane and long tail. The horn is also white, with a silvery sheen, and there is a gold chain decorating its body.

The first time this majestic, mythical creature appeared, was on the Scottish royal coat of arms, worn by William I in the 12th century. Three centuries later, their coins featured the image of this animal. It even entered the realm of religion. They believed only the Virgin Mary capable of capturing a unicorn, because only she was pure enough for the unicorn to allow itself to be caught.

Even when Georges Cuvier, a French naturalist, proved that it was impossible for unicorns to exist way back in 1825, the Scots still wouldn't have it. Cuvier claimed that a unicorn would be cloven-hoofed. This would also mean that it would have a cloven head. And if a unicorn had a cloven head, then a horn wouldn't be able to grow out of the middle of it. As simple as that.

Despite Cuvier's best efforts, the unicorn remained Scotland's national animal. They even set aside a day for it. April 9th is National Unicorn Day. Whether you believe unicorns are real or not, it seems like a fun thing to celebrate.

# Lightning Is No Joke!

Ever since the dawn of time, mankind has been curious about lightning and thunder. Even though at this point we understand how it works, it still continues to amaze us. Why? Because it's simply out of this world.

If you think of it on the local level, it may seem that lightning strikes don't even happen that often. But hold onto your seats. This one's a whopper. Lightning actually strikes the Earth about 100 times every second. Yes, you read that right. Every. Single. Second. That makes it about a 1 in 700,000 chance a person has of being struck by lightning. And with lightning bolts reaching a temperature of 50,000 degrees...I gotta tell you, I don't like those odds.

Most people aren't overly concerned about being struck by lightning. This was the case when two brothers went climbing on Moro Rock in California's Sequoia National Park, along with some other hikers. Michael and Sean McQuilken, ages eighteen and twelve, took a snapshot up there on August 20, 1975 and it turned out pretty funny, with electricity-charged air around them lifting their hair over their heads. It made one really fun picture.

Neither of them were worried. They had absolutely no idea what was coming. They even found the electricity-charged air funny. Now, almost 46 years later, Michael still remembers that deadly flash of white, the explosion, and being lifted off the ground. It all sounds too scary to be true, right? Almost like some alien invasion business.

Michael remembers how it suddenly got all cold. Then out of nowhere, it began to hail. Of course, he and his brother figured that something wasn't right, so they headed down the path, with some of the other people. But it was too late.

The lightning bolt struck. Michael bent down. When he looked up, his brother was on his knees and his back was smoking. Sean was hit directly by lightning, and he was one of three people struck. He was unconscious, completely knocked out. Later in the hospital, it was revealed he suffered third-degree burns to his back and elbows.

Luckily, both brothers survived but they learned a valuable lesson. If they had known the signs to look out for, they could have gotten to a safe place in time. Hair standing on end along with a tingling, goose-bumpy sensation of the skin, are both sure signs that lightning will strike soon.

If this happens, what should you do? Try to find shelter right away. If you can't, then squat low to the ground away from trees or anything tall. Never remain in a standing position because that makes you a bigger target and therefore, easier to strike. While squatting, do so on the balls of your feet. The point is to minimize contact with the ground. Then, only when it's safe...get the heck outta there!

# Was Alexander the Great Buried Alive?

Alexander III of Macedon, more widely known as Alexander the Great, was a king of the ancient Greek kingdom of Macedon. When he was only 20 years old, he succeeded his father King Philip II, who was assassinated during the wedding of Alexander's sister. In just 10 years, his vast kingdom stretched from Greece all the way to Northwestern India! They say his battle skills were unrivaled and he is still considered one of the most successful military leaders of all time.

Guess who Alexander's teacher was? None other than Aristotle, the Greek philosopher who himself was taught by Plato. Alexander's life was tumultuous, as was the life of many regal sons bound to inherit the throne. But there's nothing in his life still as baffling and mysterious as his death.

It was the night of June 23, when Alexander found himself at a party with his friends, after which he fell ill. Twelve days later, he died. Everyone immediately thought he was poisoned by someone working for Antipater, who was Alexander's senior officer. He had been witnessed arguing violently with the king. Strangely enough, Alexander's body didn't show any signs of decomposition for six days. Was anyone shocked? Certainly. Was anyone in disbelief? Absolutely not. Because it only strengthened what they all already believed. Alexander was not just an ordinary man. He was a god.

History experts came up with all sorts of explanations for his death. Assassination by poison, typhoid fever, malaria, and food poisoning were all offered up. But none of this could explain why his body looked intact for 6 whole days after he was pronounced dead. The only logical conclusion was the most horrific one... *Alexander wasn't dead when they buried him.*

Dr. Katherine Hall claims that most people trying to figure out how he died, focused on the wrong things. And that was the horrible fever and stomach pains he had. She offers another perspective of the king's last days. Namely, that he wasn't poisoned. He likely suffered from Guillain-Barrè Syndrome (GBS), which is a neurological disorder where your body's immune system attacks your nerves. The first symptoms are general weakness and tingling and what follows is total body paralysis.

Historical records claim that during his illness he developed a paralysis. But despite this, he remained in full control of his mental faculties right until the moment he died. This wouldn't have happened if we were poisoned. Hall believes Alexander contracted this illness from an infection of a common bacterium known as *Campylobacter pylori.*

So as the king's body was taken over by paralysis, it also meant that it needed less oxygen. In Alexander's day, doctors wouldn't be checking your heart to see if it was beating. Instead, they focused on presence or absence of breath. Seeing that the king was barely breathing, it would have been very possible that his breath was undetectable. He may have been declared dead while he was still alive!

To us, being buried alive seems like something that could never happen. But history is filled with such examples. And it just might be that Alexander the Great was one of the most famous who suffered this terrible fate.

# Over a Year Lost at Sea and Adrift
# for 6,700 Miles

More than 50 miles off the Mexican coast, the huge storm was getting worse. The terrified fisherman grabbed his radio and called for help.

"Willy! Willy! Willy! The motor is ruined!"

"Calm down, man, give me your coordinates."

"We have no GPS, it's not functioning."

"Lay an anchor."

"We have no anchor."

"Okay, we're coming to get you,"

"Come now, I am really getting (killed) out here!"

This is how it all started. But he wouldn't be found on that day. Or any of the next 437 days. Over a year later, this fisherman would wash up on a remote island beach nearly 7,000 miles away...barely alive. But still alive.

It was near the end of 2012, and Jose Salvador Alvarenga was getting his boat ready for a big fishing trip like usual. Originally from El Salvador, he was a very experienced and tested fisherman of the sea. Little did he know, leaving on this two day fishing trip, that he would not stand on dry land again until 2014!

His boat was 25 feet long and half as wide. It was completely open with no shelter and no electricity. He usually fished with his friend, Ray Perez who had helped get the boat ready for the trip. But at the last minute, Perez couldn't go. So a local 22 year old, Ezequiel Còrdoba, was offered $50 for the 2 day fishing trip.

The fishing was successful and the pair were on their way home with a crate full of fish. Then the storm hit. Being a full 50 miles away from shore, the two men still had a long way to go. The waves were knocking the boat all over the place. Huge waves would take it high up in the air and then the boat would fall and they would land with a crash. It was an incredibly scary ride and extremely hard to just stay in the boat. Falling out would mean certain death.

And then the motor died. Now they were in REAL trouble.

They threw out all of their fish to help make the boat more stable in the water and avoid capsizing. But this attracted sharks. So now they definitely couldn't fall out of the boat! They had to work incredibly hard to throw water back out of the boat. If the boat got too full of water, it would flip over and sink. When the sun set, it got cold. Really cold. The two men huddled together for warmth but thought they might freeze to death that first night. They were now completely adrift, helpless at sea.

The storm moved on but now the men had to somehow catch fish to eat without any of their equipment. Amazingly, they were able to use their hands. But it was hard work. And they nearly died from thirst as it didn't rain for two weeks. But it finally did and they were able to fill up some bottles with rain water.

After two months of living this way, floating around aimlessly in the vast Pacific Ocean, Alvarenga and Cordoba had gotten pretty good at catching fish and turtles for food. But the young Cordoba's health was failing. Tragically, the young man died. Alvarenga was devastated. He had no idea how he would survive all alone.

He almost went insane, drifting for an entire year all by himself with only his imagination to entertain him. He even had to watch dozens of large container ships cruise by him to their destinations. But they never had any workers up on their decks, so nobody ever saw him.

Finally...he saw land. He thought he was only imagining it. But he kept seeing it. He saw birds that weren't ocean birds. His ordeal was nearly over. As he drifted closer and closer, he finally slid into the water and a wave picked him up and dropped him on a sandy beach. It was the first time he had felt ground beneath him in over a year. He cried.

He didn't have any clothes on, had a big shaggy beard and crazy hair. And he was holding a knife and must have looked like a skinny bag of bones. He was quite the picture when he saw a man and woman cleaning coconuts. He had luckily washed up on a tiny island at the southern tip of the Marshall Islands, the most remote island chain in the world. If he had missed these islands, it was another 3,000 miles to the Philippines and likely that nobody would ever know what happened to Salvador Alvarenga.

He was in rough shape when he was saved. Nearly starved and full of parasites, it would take weeks in a hospital to start feeling better. But Alvarenga would hug his family again. He survived with a profound gratitude for how precious life is. And his story is one of the most remarkable ocean survival stories of all time.

# Gaylord Perry's Moon Shot

We've all heard those stories about things happening when pigs fly which means that they're not very likely to happen. At one point in history, it seemed equally absurd that someone would ever walk on the moon. And once, a guy at a baseball game even said that one particular player would never hit a home run until there was a man walking on the moon. This meant that he didn't think that baseball player had any chance of ever knocking a ball over the outfield fence.

But, first things first. The key figure in this story is Gaylord Jackson Perry who was a pitcher from North Carolina. What was he famous for? He wasn't exactly famous for his hitting, I can say that for sure. He was known for his spitball, even years after baseball rules banned it. Eventually, his pitching career landed him a well-deserved spot in the baseball Hall of Fame in 1991.

Some players remember all of their home runs, and some don't. But, when you only hit a handful over 22 years of playing, and when your first one happened just minutes after the first astronauts landed on the moon...well, you remember *that* home run, for sure.

It is said that when Perry was swinging at batting practice before a game for the San Francisco Giants, his agent Alvin Dark commented:

*They'll put a man on the Moon before he hits a homerun.*

It has become the stuff of urban legend as to who made this claim (Perry himself, his agent, or someone totally unrelated) and when (anywhere between 1962 to 1968). The truth, as always, is somewhere in between. The details are fuzzy.

The year was 1968. Perry and Dark were indeed together. Perry was taking batting practice, hitting line drives. A guy named Harry Jupiter was watching, and mentioned to Dark:

*You know, this guy has some power.*

Dark apparently laughed, with a good reply:

*Lemme tell you something. There'll be a man on the moon before he hits a homerun.*

The fateful game took place the following year. Perry was pitching against the Dodgers, when the entire world found out that Neil Armstrong walked on the moon. About twenty minutes after that, Perry came to bat in his 485th career at bat in a game, and what followed was his first and only home run.

Regardless of who said it and when, Gaylord Perry hit his first home run pretty much immediately after Neil Armstrong's foot touched the moon, marking that world famous "one small step for man, one giant leap for mankind." What a bizarre story! Now I'm left to wonder if we'll ever see those pigs flying?

# The Domino Effect

A domino effect is a chain reaction when one event starts a succession of other related events. Let's take a look at how a young woman's death in the 1880's had an impact on millions of lives and even made its way into modern pop-culture.

You probably haven't heard of Resusci Annie. She's also referred to as Rescue Annie or Resuscitation Annie. She is the CPR mannequin, who has also earned the very flattering title of "the most kissed girl in the world." These CPR mannequins have helped millions of people around the world become CPR certified and thus saved countless lives. CPR is what to do when someone can't breathe or their lungs are full of water. You close your mouth over the person's mouth who is in trouble, and blow air into their lungs.

But who is Resusci Annie? Was she just a figment of someone's imagination or did she really exist?

Her story begins more than a century ago, in the late 1880's when a body was pulled out of the river Seine in Paris, France. After a superficial glance at the mortuary, they decided that the young woman either fell into the river or jumped in herself. There were no signs of trauma on her body that would lead to the conclusion that she had been murdered.

Since they didn't know who she was, they put her body on public display in a mortuary, which was actually common practice in such cases. They hoped someone would recognize her and take her home, to be buried properly. But sadly, this never happened. Eventually, she became known only as *L'Inconnue de la Seine*, which meant the Unknown Woman of the Seine.

But this is not where her story ends. In a poetic way, her death was only the beginning, because the pathologist who conducted the autopsy was smitten by her. It was said she seemed as if she was merely asleep, like Snow White, just waiting for someone to wake her up. In an effort to preserve her peaceful face, he made a plaster *death mask* of her face which went on to be sold to thousands of people.

Seems a little weird, doesn't it? People would hang the plaster mold on a wall in their house for decoration. One author even said that an entire generation of girls in Germany did their best to look like her. Everyone found her beautiful.

In the 1950s, Archer Gordon, a member of the American Heart Association's CPR Committee, came to the conclusion that medical students needed a practice dummy for CPR (so they didn't break one another's ribs while practicing). This is where Norwegian toymaker Asmund Laerdal comes in. After seeing the lovely woman's death mask at his relative's house, he decided to use her face for the CPR dummy. And this is how Resusci Annie was born.

Still, this is not where our historical domino effect ends. Michael Jackson included the refrain "Annie, are you OK? So, Annie, are you OK? Are you OK, Annie?" in his song *Smooth Criminal,* which was a massive hit song. "Annie, are you okay?" is what people are taught to say in CPR classes before they give CPR. You want to make sure a person is unresponsive before you lock your lips on theirs! And Michael had taken a CPR class.

And this is how a completely random historical domino effect made sure that an unknown young woman would continue to live on forever, sort of...

# Were the Founding Fathers Really A Bunch of Old Guys?

Every time we hear about the United State's founding fathers, we immediately think of a bunch of old guys in a dingy old room, bent over the Declaration of Independence. That's at least what John Trumbull, a painter who painted the most famous depiction of this momentous event, showed us.

But actually, that's all wrong. Yes, those guys may have looked all wise and distinguished with their curled, white hair but don't let that fool you. I'll let you in on a little secret. All of that white hair was fake. Thomas Jefferson, who looks like someone's grandpa in that painting, was actually only 33 years old when he signed the bill. The wig was just a fashion trend, and fortunately one that died. Just imagine your parents walking around with big white wigs all the time!

The other guys were also around his age, or maybe a decade older. But not even close to the 60s looking guys we all imagine when we think of the "founding fathers".

Now, let's take a look at the 13 men who signed the bill and how old they were the moment their pens were pressed onto that piece of paper. Let's start with the first one to put his name down, John Hancock. Today, when someone wants you to sign something, it's common to say that they need your "John Hancock". It's the most famous signature ever. He was 39 when wrote his name so big that the King of England wouldn't need his glasses to read it.

Edward Rutledge, a lawyer who would later become Governor of South Carolina, was the youngest at only 26 years old. Benjamin D. Rush, who was 30, was the second youngest. Rush was a well-known physician and after signing, he went on to write an American chemistry book.

Thomas Jefferson, the man who wrote the whole thing, was 33 years old. He would, as you probably know, go on to become the third president of the United States. Arthur Middleton was only a year older than Jefferson. And Samuel Chase, a lawyer who had the distinguished position of an associate justice of the United States Supreme Court, was 35.

The bill boasted the signature of yet another lawyer, who liked to write poetry and satire in his free time, by the name of Francis Hopkinson, who was 38 when he signed.

If you know the declaration *"Give me liberty, or give me death!"* then you probably know that Patrick Henry said it. He was 40 years old and became one of the major contributors to the Bill of Rights.

John Adams was the same age as Henry, but Richard Henry Lee was slightly older. He was 44 and famous for his speech skills, which is why he became the president of Congress in 1783.

Lyman Hall was a physician and 52 years old. Samuel Adams, who helped plan the Boston Tea Party, was 53.

And, finally, Benjamin Franklin was truly a "founding father" at the ripe old age of 70. Many still consider him the most important of all those who signed, and claim that he contributed most to the declaration, which is probably what landed him on the $100 bill.

Now that we've covered all those who signed, you're probably thinking, where's the rest of the guys, like George Washington, Alexander Hamilton and James Madison? They didn't sign it simply because they were out of state. But they are most certainly considered "founding fathers" of the United States and they were young! George Washington was 35, Alexander Hamilton was just 21, and James Madison was 25. Even Betsy Ross, the lady who created the American flag, was only 25 years old when she did it.

Today, 20 year olds are not in as many leadership positions as they were when the USA was founded. The youngest member of the US senate is 40 years old, and only 9 of the 435 members of the House of Representatives are under 35 years old. And our most recent two presidents have been in their 70's when elected to lead the country. The main lesson here is that you're never too young to change the world. Many of the most important people from history were NOT old.

# Excuse Me, Have You Seen Any Vampires?

In the late 1800's, the populations of small farm towns in New England seemed to shrink as more and more people headed west searching for better soil and more opportunity. Exeter, Rhode Island was one of those towns where the number of townspeople began to dwindle. Some of them moved on to bigger cities, but was there another reason why the population was decreasing?

Between 1870-1900, Rhode Island was known as the "Vampire Capital of America." George Brown and his family lived on a small farm in Exeter. In 1883, his wife Mary became ill and died. Within 6 months, his daughter, Mary Olive, had also become sick and passed away.

A few more years passed and then his younger daughter, Mercy Brown and son Edwin had also become sick. Mercy passed away in 1892.

Edwin was a popular young store clerk in the community. A newspaper at the time was recorded saying, "If the good wishes and prayers of his many friends could be realized, friend Eddie would speedily be restored to perfect health."

The local people wanted to help save Edwin from the same fate of his mother and sisters. So they began to hypothesize about what could be making the young man so sick.

The local doctor had told Mr. Brown that his wife and children suffered from consumption, or tuberculosis. This is a disease of the lungs where those suffering seem to waste away to nothing. They have long, hard coughing fits, and become very skinny, pale and gaunt. The body seems to deteriorate over time.

The local people didn't want to believe it was tuberculosis. They had another theory. Perhaps one that could save their friend Edwin. The theory was that perhaps one of the other dead family members was actually a vampire and was leaving the grave at night and feasting on Edwin. Surely, that would explain why he seems to be slowly wasting away in front of them?

The locals got permission from Mr. Brown to exhume (dig up) the bodies of Mrs. Brown and his two daughters. They wanted to inspect and see if they could find signs of vampire life. Mrs. Brown and Mary Olive had been dead for nearly 10 years and their bodies were mostly decomposed as expected. It did not appear that they were the vampires.

Mercy Brown, on the other hand, had only been dead for 2 months when they dug up her body. It was winter and her body was still very much intact. The locals were actually pretty sure that her hair and fingernails had grown! When they examined her heart they found clotted blood. This sealed the deal. They were sure they had found their vampire.

In order to save Edwin, they had to kill the vampire that was feasting on him, so Mercy's heart and liver were burned into ashes. Just to be sure, the ashes were then mixed into Edwin's medicine. Unfortunately, the vampire theory didn't hold up and Edwin died two months later. You're shocked, right?

This isn't the only documented case of people exhuming relative's bodies searching for vampires during this time. This was happening all over New England, particularly in Rhode Island. People would dig up the body, cut off the head, and rearrange the bones. Superstition was running rampant. Experts say the 80 graves that have been discovered that have undergone these strange rituals are just the tip of the iceberg. The fear was so great, that this was a widespread practice. The victims usually suffered from tuberculosis...not vampirism!

Historians think that the local people wanted to believe they had control of their lives and were doing everything they could to help save their friends and family. Thank goodness we don't go around digging up dead bodies searching for vampires anymore!

# High Seas in High Heels?

Step aside Blackbeard. You too, Captain Jack Sparrow. The most successful pirate ever....was a woman! (But I seriously doubt she ever wore high heels.)

Pirate captains are usually ruthless, enforcing strict rules where even a small mistake might be paid for with your life. That's how they kept their operations running smoothly. At the same time, these pirate captains needed to be well versed in politics and diplomacy.

Let me introduce you to one of the most competent pirate captains ever, a lady named Ching Shih. Her fleet was exceptional and they ruled the South China Sea in the early 19th century. She alone managed to command a coalition of *thousands* of pirates. This was the largest crew that a pirate captain had EVER commanded. That's a pirate army! Then when she got bored of it all, she retired and lived the rest of her life in peace and serenity, well into her late 60s.

Shi Yang, aka Shi Xianggu, who eventually became Ching Shih (a term that means wife of Ching or Zheng, depending on the spelling), was born in 1775. She became the unofficial commander of the Guangdong Pirate Confederation, which at its peak consisted of up to 60,000 pirates on 400 junks (a type of Chinese sailing ship with fully battened sails).

There is little known about her early life. But mostly, we know that it was hard. One version is that she was a tanka, otherwise known as boat people, an ethnic group who traditionally lived on junks. She married Zheng Yi in February of 1802. This was when her life story truly began.

Zheng Yi was already an infamous pirate by that point and together with his new wife, they united five fleets into one humongous confederation which was broken up into several semi-autonomous squadrons. The leaders of these squadrons were obliged to answer to the Zhengs.

In 1807, Zheng Yi fell overboard during a particularly strong wind storm and died. His wife quickly took the reins of her now deceased husband's operations, making arrangements with the support of his nephew and a few other men she could trust.

Ching Shih enforced strict rules and a code of conduct to ensure that the crews on her ships obeyed her. When pirates performed raids, all of the plunder or stolen goods had to be registered and eighty percent of it was put into the general fund which was to benefit all the pirates. One of the most important rules Ching Shih introduced was that anyone caught stealing from the general fund would have their head cut off. That's strict! She came up with these new laws together with Chang Pao, who first became the lieutenant of her Red Flag Fleet, and eventually her second husband.

During her reign, she made sure to keep good relationships with all leaders in her fleet which wasn't easy at all. She did this by supervising everything that was happening. She had quite a knack for warfare and was clever in her strategies. She was known to kidnap Chinese officials, blockade important water passages and cause general chaos for the Chinese government.

The Chinese government eventually stopped trying to defeat the large pirate regime and started trying to negotiate with them. This is when Ching Shih really showed her intelligence and negotiating skills.

Ching Shih knew that most pirates died at a young age, usually in brutal ways. She also knew that wasn't what she wanted for herself. So in 1810, Ching Shih worked up a very clever agreement with the Chinese government. She turned herself in. The arrangement was that she and any pirate who surrendered with her would receive full amnesty and be pardoned for all of their crimes. They got to keep all of their stolen treasure and many of the pirates received jobs working for the government.

She made sure that Chang Pao would get to keep anywhere between 20 and 30 vessels to continue his salt trade. Unfortunately, Chang Pao died when he was only 36 years old. Ching Shih lived to a ripe old age of 69 and she enjoyed every moment of it as one of the few successful pirate captains to not be killed at sea.

# That's the King's Pigeon Poop!

Think of something you find really annoying. For me, it's just walking down the street, without a care in the world, then splat! Pigeon poop! Whether it gets on me or I have to dodge stepping in it, it's just downright gross.

You see pigeons everywhere. Some people even call them flying rats. They tend to spread disease. And they're not even that cute. Despite their nasty habit of pooping everywhere, pigeons have actually benefited mankind immensely. For example, pigeon poop (also known as guano) is rich in nitrogen, which makes it a great fertilizer. This means that the domestication of pigeons resulted in growing better crops, so in a way, pigeons are partly responsible for the betterment of humankind. Weird, but true.

That's not all. Pigeon poop didn't only help agriculture develop, but also King George I of England proclaimed that all pigeon droppings were the property of the British Crown. Sounds silly, but he actually had a good reason.

You see, pigeon poop contains saltpeter. Of course, it's not a guy called Peter who fell into a batch of salt. It's actually one of the three main ingredients of gunpowder, also known as potassium nitrate. They would take pigeon poop, extract saltpeter from it, then mix it with the other two ingredients, which are charcoal and sulphur, and voila! You've got gunpowder. And whoever had gunpowder back in the day, had all the power.

Do you see the importance of pigeon poop to the British Crown now? Gunpowder was crucial in warfare where you had guns and cannons, which means that in the historical context, pigeon poop was invaluable. Even priceless. More important than gold. It was so popular at some point, that the British kings hired armed guards to prevent people from stealing pigeons.

However, saltpeter could also be found in caves, so saltpeter mining was considered to be one of the first major industries of the new frontier. Eventually, with the emergence of new technologies, pigeon poop was left alone and factories started producing all the necessary ingredients of gunpowder.

Finally, pigeons could breathe (and poop!) in peace.

# Take This Mold Juice And Call Me In the Morning

The discovery of penicillin was basically the dawn of a whole new era. How? Because before penicillin, hospitals were full of people whose cuts and scratches got so severely infected that all doctors could do was to wait and hope. Not to mention the fact that infections such as pneumonia or rheumatic fever were completely untreatable at that point. Penicillin changed all of this. But did you know that Alexander Fleming initially called it mold juice?

Fleming had a great education, which led him to study at St. Mary's Hospital under Almroth Wright, who was actually the bacteriologist who discovered the typhoid vaccine. If you have a great mentor, you might be bound to do great things yourself. And, that's exactly what happened.

During WWI, Fleming worked in a military hospital in France. Surprisingly, his main concern wasn't people dying of their battle wounds, but actually from wounds they got in the trenches that would get infected. Fleming tried to stop and prevent infection with different antiseptic procedures, but none of them proved successful because these strong chemicals ended up destroying both the healthy and the infected tissue.

Then, after WWI, Fleming went back to St. Mary's, and one fortunate accident led to one of the most important discoveries in the field of medicine. At this point, Fleming was a successful physician and scientist, but his laboratory was a bit of a mess. It was creative chaos. Not something you'd expect of a scientist, right?

Below his laboratory, there was a mycology lab, where other scientists would experiment with fungus and mold. When Fleming went on his summer vacation, the unusually hot London weather allowed the mold spores to drift up to his laboratory and reproduce there. Upon his return, he started cleaning up a bit, and then he saw it. A small petri dish where he was experimenting with staphylococci bacteria was a total mess. It was contaminated by something else. There were some funky, fuzzy growths in there. It looked dreadful, and anyone apart from Fleming would have probably thrown it away. But his trained eye saw something interesting. There was a light green mold on top of the petri dish and around it, there was a clean area. This could only mean one thing. The mold was somehow destroying the bacteria. Amazing!

He eventually discovered this was *Penicillium notatum,* which is Latin for a small brush. But other doctors and scientists would often jokingly refer to it as mold juice. Even though Fleming provided the world with priceless new tools in humanity's war against disease, he remained modest, saying "My only merit is that I did not neglect the observation."

So, the next time your mom tells you to clean up your room because it's a mess, tell her you're waiting for a monumental discovery to fall into your lap. Not even mom logic can beat Fleming's. Hmmm, actually I'm not at all sure of that one. You should probably listen to your Mom no matter what!

# This Masterpiece Stinks

If you ever visit the Vatican in Italy you will gaze in awe at the ceiling of the Sistine Chapel. It is considered the cornerstone work of High Renaissance art, commissioned by Pope Julius II and painted by the one and only Michaelangelo between 1508 and 1512.

The elaborate paintings consist of various elements, all of which are parts of other great works of art, such as the fresco The Last Judgment, and other paintings by Botticelli, Domenico Ghirlandaio, Raphael and others. There are nine scenes from the Book of Genesis, of which The Creation of Adam is the most famous. Basically, it's a wonderful work of art which has served as a guideline for many painters later on. It's an art legend!

You would think that Michaelangelo would have been ecstatic to paint it. After all, he was doing what he did best and what he enjoyed most, right? Well, not so much as it turns out. Some historical sources claim that he wasn't too happy to take on this job. In fact, he even wrote a poem on how much he hated doing it.

You see, in addition to being a fantastic painter and sculptor, he also dabbled in poetry a little. Of course he did, he was a Renaissance man. So it was easy for him to transfer his irritation onto paper, and complain about how slow the work was going, how difficult it was, and how he felt inadequate to do it justice.

He mentions, among other things: *"My stomach's squashed under my chin... my haunches are grinding into my guts...*

*Every gesture I make is blind and aimless... Because I'm stuck like this, my thoughts are crazy... My painting is dead... I am not a painter."*

As you can see, he actually believed it was no good! He even went as far as to refuse the title of painter, something he'd been proud of before that. The poem is filled with thoughts of impatience, stress and total irritation. It seems a bit silly that the poem about one of the greatest artistic works in all of history isn't about praising it, but actually whining. Genius or not, Michelangelo was sometimes all too human, just like the rest of us.

Eventually, this job immortalized him. So it might be helpful to remember that even when you don't want to do something, try doing it anyway. You might end up being remembered for it until the end of time.

# Just A Kid

Kids are not typically involved in politics. That's because they usually aren't given the chance. But kids are capable of amazing things. All grown ups need to do is allow kids to ask questions, even if there's a million of them...and just learn to listen.

One little girl who made a difference because she was allowed to make her voice known is Samantha Reed Smith. She lived in a time when the US and the Soviet governments started doing extensive research on developing weapons that could be launched from satellites. Immediately, anti-nuclear protests started taking place all around the globe and this was where little Samantha (who was just 10 years old at the time) decided to write a letter to none other than Soviet leader Yuri Andropov. All she wanted to know was why the Soviet Union and the United States were acting so aggressively towards each other:

Dear Mr. Andropov,

My name is Samantha Smith. I am 10 years old. Congratulations on your new job. I have been worrying about Russia and the United States getting into a nuclear war. Are you going to vote to have a war or not? If you aren't please tell me how you are going to help to not have a war. This question you do not have to answer, but I would like it if you would. Why do you want to conquer the world or at least our country? God made the world for us to share

110

*and take care of. Not to fight over or have one group of*
*people own it all. Please let's do what he wanted and have*
*everybody be happy too.*
*Samantha Smith*

I doubt that any grown up could have summed up
more perfectly what everyone was thinking than what
came from the heart of this ten year old girl. In this
day and age, you can contact anyone online. It was
actually a very far-fetched idea back in the 1980s that
her letter would reach Andropov and even more, that
he would actually read it and reply (important people
usually had others to do these kinds of jobs for them).

Samantha's letter was published in the Russian
newspapers. But there was no reply and little Samantha wanted one. So she went ahead and contacted the
Soviet Union's Ambassador to the United States, just
to ask if she would be getting a reply or not. And sure
enough, a reply followed.

Andropov thanked her for the letter, and compared
her to Tom Sawyer's friend Becky, who was just like
Samantha, an honest and brave girl. He assured her
that they were doing their best so that there wouldn't
be a nuclear war, and reminded her that everyone wanted the same thing...peace.

Then, he even went so far as to invite her over:
*"I invite you, if your parents will let you, to come to our*
*country, the best time being this summer. You will find*
*out about our country, meet with your contemporaries,*
*visit an international children's camp – Artek – on the*

*sea. And see for yourself: in the Soviet Union, everyone is for peace and friendship among peoples."*

Samantha went for a visit and had a lovely time. She became known as a Goodwill Ambassador, the youngest there ever was. And even after her visit to the Soviet Union, she continued to take part in peacemaking activities. Tragically, she died at the age of thirteen in a plane crash. But that only goes to show you that no matter how short your life is, you can always strive to make a difference.

# The Cobra Effect

Have you ever been in a situation where you are working hard to solve a problem, but actually ended up making the problem worse? That's the cobra effect!

While this might sound like some cool karate move (I can totally see a kick called the cobra effect), it's not. The cobra effect is a term used by people studying human and business relationships. The cobra effect starts as an incentive, or something that motivates you to do something or act in a certain way. But a cobra effect incentive has a result which is neither planned nor expected, and is usually something terrible.

Why is it called the cobra effect when it seems that this idea has nothing to do with cobras? We have Hors Siebert, a German economist, to thank for coming up with the name. He based it on a funny (well, it wasn't funny at the time) event which happened in India while it was still a British colony.

There were loads of venomous cobras in Delhi (the capital city), and that was obviously a BIG problem. Many died from snake bites, and people were generally afraid, especially because it was easy for snakes to get inside houses. The British government thought long and hard about possible solutions and they eventually came up with one. They'd just pay people for every dead cobra they bring in, hoping to get people to do the killing themselves, thus lowering the snake numbers. Sounds like a good plan, right?

In the beginning, sure. People kept bringing dead cobras and getting good money for them. The numbers were actually starting to go down. But then, it seems that the British government neglected to take into account the element of human cleverness. You see, it wasn't enough to just kill wild snakes. Some people actually started breeding cobras, which they would then kill and get money for. It didn't cost much to breed the snakes so you could still make good money by just raising them yourself and then killing them.

The government found out eventually, and they stopped the whole deal. No more money for dead snakes. Forget about it. What did the cobra breeders do with the snakes?

This is where the whole plan went bust, because the breeders took all the snakes and just released them into the wild. Now the cobra population was even higher than before! So not only was the problem not solved, but it had been made even worse.

There are many other examples of this throughout history. You may even have some examples in your own life. So today, the cobra effect and its impact on problems and solutions is still studied. It helps people to dig a little deeper into the unexpected consequences of their decisions.

# That Time A Best Selling Book Was Written by a 9 Year Old

A kid's imagination can be endless. Pirates, princesses, castles, and sword fights are just some of the many ideas that kids have whirling through their heads at any point in their day. But did you know that one kid actually used her incredible imagination and wrote a book, which eventually became a bestseller? Not only that, she was just nine years old when she wrote it!

Little Daisy Ashford, whose real name was Margaret Mary Julia Ashford, was born in 1881 in Petersham, London. She had five siblings, and all of them were homeschooled by their mother, Emma. Daisy had always been a story teller, and an avid book reader. Her father's library was filled with books that dealt with important issues of that time, such as social class, women's rights and so on. Little Daisy read all of them, and later retold those same issue through a child's lens in her book called The Young Visiters (no, it's not a typo - the publishers actually chose to keep Daisy's spelling of all words, because they believed it added to the mystery of a child's mind).

She dictated her first story to her father when she was only four, and wrote this book at age nine. But she didn't show it to anyone at the time. She just tucked it into her drawer, where the book was left hidden until

27 years later. Daisy's friend Margaret Mackenzie was sick, and Daisy, being the good friend that she was, gave her the manuscript.

Margaret thought it was very amusing, so she gave it to some other friends of hers, and as these things usually go, one thing led to another. Eventually, Daisy's book was finally published in 1919.

The publishers didn't make a single change to the book. As you can tell, even the title has a typo, but they left it like that. JM Barrie, who wrote *Peter Pan*, wrote the preface. Because of this, many thought that this was just a trick Barrie was playing on everyone, making them believe that a kid wrote it...while in fact, it was him.

But it wasn't a trick. It was actually a little literary work of art, written by a nine year old girl with a passion for the written word and an eye for detail. She wrote a society novel about people in the Victorian era, and what their daily struggles were regarding class and proper courtship. While most other kids her age would write stories about princesses and magic, she chose reality. And that made her book so interesting to read for adults. But JM Barrie did pretty well writing about a flying boy who wouldn't grow up and was always fighting pirates. So you never know!

# Accidental Inventions

Just imagine all the little pleasures in life that make it so much sweeter and easier. If something breaks, you can super glue it. Feeling like you want to nibble on something? Eat potato chips. Feeling bored? Pop bubble wrap. Need to build a campfire? Duh. Light a match. Your food got cold? Easy. Just microwave it. I mean, the list is endless.

People must have worked long hours on these inventions so we could use them now, right? Wrong. All of these (plus so many more) are accidental discoveries. Yes, that's right. Chips and chocolate chip cookies were an accident. A blessed accident, but an accident nonetheless. Let's see how some of them came to be.

Let's start with the matches. You'd think someone purposefully worked on finding portable fire, right? Well, not really. A chemist named John Walker accidentally got a stick coated in some chemical compounds close to his fire. The stick immediately went ablaze. He called them friction lights, and first made them out of cardboard, only later moving to wood splints and sandpaper. And voila! Friction lights turned into matches.

How about tea bags? That one sounds pretty straightforward. Thomas Sullivan was your go to guy in 1908 for tea services. Because there were so many tea varieties, he figured he could send samples of different flavors in small, silk pouches. They actually weren't meant to be used at all. He expected people to take the tea out when preparing it, but people got lazy and just dipped the whole thing into boiling water, and there you have it. Good ole tea bags.

Potato chips. We all love them, but did you know they were the genius result of one angry chef? It was a warm summer in 1853. George Crum, a well known chef, had just served a customer some French fries. The customer then returned them, asking for thinner and crispier fries. It was said that Crum, who was already in a bad mood, got even angrier and cut those potatoes super thin, then fried them until they were super crunchy. Imagine his shock when the customer loved them! Some have disputed this one as just a legend.

What about the well known drink, by the name of Coca-Cola? John Pemberton made Pemberton's French Wine Coca in the form of a syrup, made from wine and coca extract. He sold it as medicine for nervous ailments. Then, in 1885, alcohol was banned, and Pemberton had to modify his syrup. He substituted the wine with carbonated water and sold it as the brain tonic we now know as Coca Cola.

We all love chewing gum, but it actually didn't start off as something you were supposed to have in your mouth. Thomas Adams Sr. was using chicle, a natural gummy substance produced by certain trees to create rubber for tires. That failed, but he realized it was perfectly edible and began to market it as chewing gum. Some evidence points out that northern Europeans were chewing bark 9,000 years ago to relieve tooth-aches. The Aztecs did it too, but only kids and single women could chew it in public, while married women and widows had to chew it in private. Go figure.

Popsicles. This one is so ingenious that it must have been a kid who created it. And it was! Frank Epperson, an 11 year old kid, played around with some soda powder and water, mixing it all together. Then, he left the stirrer inside the concoction in the freezer, and went about his business, forgetting about it until the following day. When he went to check on it, he tried it and to his surprise, it didn't taste half bad. He called it the Epsicle, combining the word icicle with his name. That didn't stick around, so he changed it to Popsicle. And the rest is history.

There are so many more of these accidental inventions and discoveries, and it only goes to show you that sometimes accidents can have very happy outcomes!

# The 80's Called and They Want Their Phones Back

Just imagine all the cool stuff you can find at the beach. Coins. Rings. Bottles. Seashells. But Garfield toy phones? Come on.

For the last 35 years, there's been an unsolved mystery of these orange colored toy phones with the image of the lasagna loving cat, Garfield, washing up on the shores of France. Garfield was a famous newspaper comic. You may know all about him, there was a TV show, a movie, and so on.

This story begins in the 1980s, when Garfield rose to fame. His image was everywhere; stickers, toys, shirts, even Garfield phones! Then, all of a sudden, whole toy phones and smaller parts of them started appearing on French beaches, as if that lazy cat's smug grin was taunting everyone: *Hey! Hey, you! Try to guess what I'm doing here?* And a few people took this question seriously, determined to find the answer. It took them about 35 years, but by golly, they found it.

Around 200 of these toy phones were found on the coastline every year. This meant that something serious was happening below the ocean waters, and it was probably a pollution hazard.

A farmer got in touch with the French environmental activist group called Ar Vilantsou, to tell them about his strange find. He had discovered a metal shipping container in the back of a sea cave. And inside it? Garfield toy phones!

The cave was mostly inaccessible because of the tides but at their first chance, the activists immediately headed over. They were astonished to see bits and pieces of Garfield phones and metal from the container everywhere around the cave. As was to be expected, most of the debris had already washed ashore. They took care of the leftovers, figuring that the container somehow washed up into the cave after a storm, and the ocean tried to clean itself, by expelling bits of the phones little by little.

This is a great lesson in trying to reduce the amount of plastic waste in our lives so it doesn't wind up in the ocean or washed up on beaches like Garfield.

As for our orange cat friend, these phones remain a novelty, especially when Garfield opens its eyes when you pick up the receiver. When the receiver is put back down, Garfield decides it's nap time again. Maybe we should start collecting them. Who knows? They might go up in value soon now that they're no longer mysteriously greeting French beachgoers.

# You Were Captured
# By Who? HOW?

Hussars. These were brave warriors whose daredevil tactics were the stuff of legend. Although considered a light cavalry, they could do things that made entire kingdoms tremble in fear.

They first appeared somewhere around the 14th century, consisting of Serb warriors who crossed over into southern Hungary. Under the king of Hungary, they were trained using spears, swords and shields. Eventually, after the 16th century they became a well known light cavalry with the use of firearms.

As time went by, other European countries realized something: *Hey, these Hussar guys can really fight. Maybe we should get in on the action?* So their military formation was adopted in other countries as well.

But what made these guys so special? Well, apart from other feats, they managed to capture an entire Dutch fleet out at sea. Horses vs. ships doesn't seem very fair, right? But the hussars didn't even flinch at the idea. And they did it without resorting to a single shot.

Let's see what all the commotion was about. The French Revolution took place in the late 1700s. France said no more monarchy, and pushed for a republican government. This made all other European countries tremble with fear that these revolutionary ideas might

spread. Britain, Spain, Portugal and the Dutch Republic tried to invade France and put an end to this. The French fought bravely, and not only did they manage to defend themselves successfully, but they actually went on the offense.

They hit the Republic of the Seven United Netherlands in December 1795. The Netherlands consisted of many islands, and even though they entered the capital city itself, there was still much to do. The Dutch navy was anchored near the island port of Den Helder island. Only the winter was very harsh, with many bodies of water freezing over, so the Dutch navy fleet got stuck in the ice between two islands.

The residents of Den Helder were on the French side, and told the French all about the fleet of frozen ships. Within days, the 8th Hussar Regiment and the 15th Line Infantry Regiment of the French Revolutionary Army spread out all over the ice (the bay was shallow and the ice solid enough) to create a balance. Slowly, they got near the fleet.

According to the legend of this bizarre tale of horses vs. ships, the Hussar cavalry covered their horses' hooves in fabric so they wouldn't make noise on the ice. Each horse carried two soldiers so they would overpower the sleeping crews. The ice was thick and did not break under the weight of all those horses.

Thanks to the sneak attack, all 14 ships were taken over easily and without much fuss. Not a single soldier died. There were no casualties for either side. On that cold January night in 1795, 14 war ships were captured by a cavalry on horseback. That's not something that has happened too often!

# It's Space Metal, Dude

People have always been curious about stuff falling from the sky. Why wouldn't we be? You just look up at all those stars, wondering about so many things. But it seems ancient cultures in Greenland weren't simply wondering about the stars. They actually discovered a fallen meteorite and decided to put it to good use and make tools from it...1,200 years ago! And, this was even before Norse settlers from Iceland came to Greenland, bringing iron.

Greenland is one of the largest frozen areas in the world. There's just ice and snow as far as the eye can see. The first people lived there around 2500 BC, and they were followed by the first Paleo-Eskimo cultures, anywhere between 2500 BC and 800 BC. These prehistoric hunters didn't have to wait for Norse settlers to come bringing iron. They used what they had on hand, plunging them into the aptly named Meteorite Age, during which they mined metal from space rocks. Awesome, right?

So what really happened? It is generally believed that the meteorite crashed on Earth, falling somewhere in the area of the Cape York Peninsula in northwest Greenland, about 10,000 years ago. The whole thing was huge, so upon impact, it split into at least 8 extremely large pieces.

Seeing how much people love naming things, these chunks also got names. The biggest one was known as

Ahighito (The Tent) and it weighed approximately 31 tons. Then there was The Man, weighing in at 22 tons, The Woman a 2.5 ton piece and The Dog, a mini-mass of only half a ton.

All of these fragments are now safely kept at the American Museum of Natural History. This is where it gets interesting. Archaeologists discovered that the Paleo-Eskimos were actually chipping off fragments from these humongous boulders and making all sorts of things from them, such as knives or harpoon blades.

It seems that back then, nothing was wasted. The blacksmiths knew exactly what to do with these big chunks. First, they would knock off a smaller piece, then beat it totally flat, making sure to create a sharp edge. Then they would keep hardening it into an arrowhead or knife. They even traded these weapons. Some of these tools were even found in Canada.

How did archaeologists know that these pieces were made from that meteor? Simple. The meteor has a unique chemical signature, among other things it has a lot of nickel. So the chemical make-up of the meteor matches the chemical make-up of the tools. Pretty cool to be able to tell that these tools and weapons were made out of a giant rock that fell from the sky!

# A Bizarre Scientific Mystery

Science is amazing. We know why the Earth revolves around the Sun. We know why we fall down to the ground instead of floating up into the air. We know what makes us sick and how to protect ourselves from those nasty little germs. We know which part of our brain is responsible for movement, speech, etc. And yet, scientists have NO answer to a very simple question... how does a bicycle keep going without tipping over?

Seems like such an easy looking thing to explain, right? But apparently it's not. At least people generally agree on one thing. Every bicycle has two wheels, right? Unless it's a unicycle. Or a tricycle. But let's just focus on the bicycle this time. Two wheels means two gyroscopes. A gyroscope is basically a sphere that keeps spinning very quickly, creating a force which makes it easy to keep going forward. Changing its orientation is the tricky part.

However, if you lean left or right, you make a change to the spinning. You change the horizontal axis, so that push changes into a turning motion instead of spinning. The result is of course simple and pretty obvious. You lean left, you turn left. The same goes for the right. This, my friends, is called precession.

You can try an experiment of your own. Just take your bike and push it. It will keep going in the direction it was pushed, right? But if you try running alongside the moving bike, and you push it in a different direction, it will either fall if you push it too hard, or it will realign itself and change direction, then keep going. Amazing, right?

This means that while these gyroscopes are very important for the movement of a bicycle, it is actually the rider who does most of the work and decides on the speed and the direction of the motion. But you knew that already. The rider needs to steer, position his or her body properly and always keep at a certain speed so as not to fall. This is what we're all trying to master when we first learn how to ride a bicycle. Once you know the basics, you can easily do the no-hands ride, but...it's important to understand that the gyroscopic action becomes more important than your body. You're relying on the first wheel to maintain a straight path, because your hands aren't steering.

So basically, cycling is a balancing skill, with a little help from gyroscopic force. But why don't they tip over when we ride? There is still no concrete scientific explanation. And that's confusing because it seems so simple. You spin the wheels and just use your balance. But that doesn't really put a neat and tidy bow on it. The truly astounding fact here is that scientists can explain to you why a plane can fly without falling but *not* why a bicycle can ride without tipping over. It's truly a crazy world.

# Is It Breezy In Here?

The first Olympic games started in ancient Greece in the early 8th century BC. If the modern Olympic Games followed ancient tradition, then we would be covering our eyes and referring to the Olympics as the Naked Games. No joke.

There's indisputable proof that during the ancient Olympic Games participants were naked. Plato left writings of it, Homer's Iliad also mentions this custom, and even a few drawings from that time confirm this. Yikes! This means that they did everything naked. Wrestling, boxing, horse racing, you name it. They would be naked, gleaming from only the olive oil that covered their bodies. It was customary for athletes to anoint themselves with the oil before participating.

But, I guess we should have expected that. That is, if we know what the word gymnastics really means. It is based on the Greek adjective gymnos, which means lightly-clad or naked. See? It's in the name itself! But it's hardly our fault for not being fluent in ancient Greek.

So where did this tradition come from? There are a few theories. One is that a Spartan runner named Acanthus started it by just appearing without his loincloth. Another version attributes it to Osippus, who won a foot race while running naked, realizing that he could run faster without his loincloth. Go figure. The third version states that one runner tripped over his loincloth when it slipped down from his waist and fell. That's called bad luck. Later, a magistrate who was in charge of the games made it official that all athletes would compete naked from then on.

One historian named Thucydides wrote around the 5th century BC, that Spartans loved playing the games naked because they loved showing themselves off. It had something to do with initiation rites. You know, boys walking around naked and then doing something awe-inspiring to become men. But in reality, nudity was fundamental to Greek culture. They believed that only barbarians refused to show their god-given bodies, and athletes proudly strutted their stuff up and down the stadium.

So the next time you're watching the Olympic Games, be grateful for the oncoming of civilization. Otherwise, we'd be watching naked, oily people running and jumping around.

# You Do What?

We all know it is hard to get up in the morning for school or work. Admit it. Sometimes, you just hit that snooze button, buying yourself those precious 5 minutes. Or you wish your parents had a snooze button. If only!

In today's modern times, it's easy to set your phone or alarm clock to wake you up exactly when you need to get out of bed. But what did people do in the old days, when they didn't have alarm clocks? Simple. They had knocker-uppers.

While the term sounds funny (and it most definitely is), knocker-uppers were a very important part of Britain during the 19th century and the first part of the 20th century. As their name suggests, they were basically people who would knock on your window at an exact pre-arranged time to wake you up. This was very useful for people who had to wake up very early and go to work.

Knocker-uppers would initially ring the doorbell or knock loudly. After all, the point was to wake up the entire house, right? But the down side of this was that sometimes, other houses nearby would be woken up too. So knocker-uppers switched to long sticks with a knob on the end. There were also soft hammers, rattles, and even pea shooters. The point was to reach the bedroom window which was often located at the top floor of the house, without waking up the house next door. The knocker-uppers would rap a few times, wait for the window to be opened, signaling that the man or the lady of the house were awake, and then the knocker-upper would move on to their next customer's window.

The pay wasn't much but every little bit helps, right? They were paid around a shilling per week, by a single customer. This amounts to around 12 cents. Of course, there would be those who "forgot" to pay the knocker-upper and their window would be left out of the morning roll call, leading them to be late for work.

There is even a fun tongue-twister popular at the time to honor the profession:

*We had a knocker-up, and our knocker-up had a knocker-up,*

*And our knocker-up's knocker up didn't knock our knocker up,*

*So our knocker-up didn't knock us up,*

*'Cos he's not up.*

Try saying *that* quickly.

With the appearance of electricity and affordable alarm clocks, knocker-uppers became obsolete, although in some parts of Britain and Ireland they continued with their line of work as late as the 1970s.

# Excuse Me?
# A Little Help Down Here?

The Victorian Era was a time of few medical technologies. Surgeries were done minus the anesthesia, (ouch!) medicine was hit or miss, and worst of all, diagnoses were sometimes so wrong that a live person would be pronounced dead and then buried!

While it seems like something out of the scary movie, it's actually true. These things really happened. People were buried alive. More than once! It was actually what Victorians were most frightened of. I mean, how hard is it to know for sure whether someone is dead or alive? Seems pretty easy, right? Well, back then all they knew to go on was smell and touch.

This was the time of cholera outbreaks and infections which would leave you constipated (or even worse, with diarrhea) and dehydrated. Some people were so sick that they looked dead, although they were alive. And just pressing a hand on their chest to see if their heart was beating was usually the only way doctors knew to check. And sometimes, they were wrong and a person was buried alive!

Essie Dunbar, for example, was lucky enough to escape such a fate. She suffered from epilepsy, and had what seemed to be a fatal attack in 1915. The doctors declared her dead, and the funeral arrangements were immediately made. Her sister who lived out of town, wanted to see her one last time but she was late for the funeral. By the time she arrived, Essie was already buried. Her sister demanded that the coffin be dug up, so she could say goodbye to Essie. Once this was done, Essie sat up and started coughing. She lived for another 47 years!

Another famous case of premature burial happened in 1937, when 19 year old Angelo Hays got into a horrible motorcycle accident. He ran into a brick wall, headfirst. Reports state he was in such a bad condition that even his parents weren't allowed to see him. There was no pulse, so doctors declared him dead. Shortly after, he was buried. Then, a local insurance company conducted an investigation, and his body needed to be exhumed. Imagine their surprise when they realized that Hays' body was still warm to the touch! Apparently, he was in a coma after the accident and his body needed less oxygen to survive. This was what kept him alive! He had many surgeries and spent much time in rehabilitation, but he lived for another 40 years.

So, the clever Victorians came up with a safety coffin. It's meant to save you from a whole lot of pain. This safety coffin had everything you'd want to be comfortable. It had cotton padding, feeding tubes, escape hatches, and eventually...a cord attached to a bell outside. But being buried a few feet underground meant that you needed air to stay alive, and this was a bit tricky with these coffins.

The bell system proved to be the best option as escape hatches tended to be kind of hard to use if you're struggling for air in a coffin. The bell system was created by Dr. Johann Gottfried Taberger. It was basically a string connected to a bell above ground on one side, and the hands and feet of the buried person on the other. So if you woke up in a coffin and realized that you had been buried alive, all you needed to do was pull that string and the bell would ring, signaling to the cemetery watchman that you're still alive and kicking down there.

However, even back then they knew of the decay process (a corpse releases gas and swells up in the coffin before disintegrating), and sometimes the bell would be activated accidentally when the dead body swelled. Still, every time a bell rang in the cemetery, they went running for the shovels.

Thank goodness modern medicine has advanced and we can actually tell if people are dead or not!

# That's No Ordinary Dog

When you see a little Yorkshire Terrier who weighs only 4 pounds and stands only 7 inches tall, you'd never think this little cutie pie could bravely go on jungle combat missions and even jump from a plane with a custom doggie parachute! And yet, this is exactly what Smokey did.

Smokey was a brave little dog who served in World War II. It was in February of 1944 that an American soldier found little Smokey hiding in an abandoned foxhole in the New Guinea jungle. The soldiers figured she belonged to some Japanese soldiers, but when given orders in either Japanese or English, she didn't seem to understand either language. She was already full-grown when found, and the soldier who found her had no use for her. He sold her to Corporal Willie A. Wynne for two Australian pounds, which was about $6.44 at the time, because that was exactly how much the soldier owed for losing a poker game.

This is where little Smokey's adventure truly began. She fought bravely by Wynne's side, neatly tucked into his backpack. She suffered heat and humidity, she walked on rough coral for months without developing any paw-related illnesses (which other war dogs often got), she ate whatever Wynne had to share with her. She bravely went into twelve combat missions and she was awarded eight battle stars. She even jumped from 30 feet with a mini parachute made just for her. She always slept in Wynne's tent on a blanket that was also made just for her, out of a green felt card table cover.

Wynne said that she saved his life, referring to her as his little *angel from a foxhole*. She warned him to duck for cover, saving him from incoming shells which took out eight men that were behind him.

She learned many tricks, and loved to entertain troops both during their missions as well as in hospitals. Becoming a hero in her own right, she helped with building an airbase, by performing the grueling work of several days in only a few minutes. She ran with a telegraph wire through a 70 foot long pipe which was only 8 inches in diameter. She was scared and uncertain, and even turned back once, but hearing Wynne's voice on the other end made her courageous enough to go through with it. Her feat meant that builders didn't have to dig for three days to place the wire. Little Smokey was patted and praised for five whole minutes after her effort.

When they returned home to the States after the war, they were treated like rock stars. Everyone wanted an interview and Smokey became a national sensation. They continued to entertain the masses on TV, but also at veterans' hospitals.

She died in 1957, around the age of 14. Wynne buried her in a WWII .30 caliber ammo box. Fifty years later, she even got a lifesize statue of herself sitting in a GI helmet. The dedication reads: "Smoky, the Yorkie Doodle Dandy, and the Dogs of All Wars." It seems that dogs truly are a man's best friend.

# Take This Job and Shove It

Think of the worst job in the world. Which one do you think it is? A retail salesperson on Christmas Eve? Grave digger? Manual sewer worker? While those jobs might have a bit of unpleasantness, they are still far from the worst. That prestigious title goes to the Groom of the Stool.

The name itself explains it. The Groom of the Stool was basically responsible for taking care of King Henry VIII's toilet needs. This included supplying water, towels and a washbowl to wash the king's behind when he was done with his business. Some historians believe the wiping part was done by the grooms, while others think the king wasn't really that lazy.

In addition to this, the grooms had to closely monitor the king's bowel movements, pay attention to the king's diet, and even check the waste for possible signs of illness or decreasing health. All this was done so that they could all be assured that the king was in good health and able to rule the kingdom.

Today, taking care of such business is very, VERY private. We don't like to have an audience, but it was different back in the Tudor age. The king's bedroom had a waste closet, and a so-called privy chamber. This special room was attended by several people, and the head of all of them was the Groom of the Stool.

Eventually, the Groom of the Stool took on even more duties (or should we say doodies?), by helping the king dress and undress, dictate the king's diet, and similar. He could even say that someone wasn't welcome in the king's private chambers, and the king would obey.

While this job sounds a bit...gross, it still had its upsides, too. For example, whenever the king traveled, the Groom of the Stool traveled with him being granted comfy lodgings. He would also get the king's old clothes and furnishings. They might be second hand, but just think of all the fine silk the king's dressed in. Not too shabby. Sometimes, if they wanted a meeting with the king, people would have to go through the Groom of the Stool who could decide yay or nay in favor of a person. Basically, if you wanted to be on the king's good side, you had to be on his groom's good side as well.

When Elizabeth I became queen, it was considered improper for a man to attend to her private needs (with good reason), so a new position was created: the Lady of the Bedchamber. She had all the duties of the Groom of the Stool.

Eventually, the position was abolished. I guess even kings and queens realized that they needed to wipe their own behinds.

# This Story Smells!

One of the most impossible fortresses in the world to break into is the Bank of England. It was built with walls that are 8 feet thick. It's quite old for a bank and has been around since 1694. It holds the 2nd biggest amount of gold in one place in the entire world. It's been right in the middle of downtown London on Threadneedle Street since 1734. The bank is extremely proud of its history. It has never been broken into or robbed. Well, it hasn't been broken into by thieves. But there was that one time that an honest sewer worker was able to sneak in...

The year was 1836. The bank directors had gotten a mysterious letter. The writer of the letter said that he could get as much gold as he wanted out of the main gold vault because he had complete access to it. The directors thought that was really funny. London is full of strange people and one of them either had a funny sense of humor or they were crazy.

Weeks went by and they got another letter. It made the same claims as the first and offered to meet the directors inside the gold vault at a specific time of their choice. They were interested enough to play along. I might have been concerned that it was a scary Batman villain like the Joker. But nobody had heard of Batman back then.

So the directors set a time for this mysterious letter writer to meet them in the gold vault. I'm sure they must have felt a little silly for agreeing to this. But sure enough, right at the time that they had agreed to meeting, they heard a noise underneath them. And then a man popped out of the floor! The directors couldn't believe their eyes.

The man worked in the London sewer system. He had been making an inspection during sewage repairs that led to his discovery. He had found an old passageway that led him directly underneath one of the biggest collections of gold in the world. Thank goodness he wasn't a Batman villain, or the gold would have already been long gone. But just to make sure, the directors immediately checked to make sure that no gold was missing.

Much to their relief, it was all there. They gave the friendly sewer inspector a nice reward of 800 British pounds. In 1836, this would be like getting $80,000 today. Not too shabby! To this day, we have no idea what the name of this sewer worker was. But most believe (including the Bank of England) that this is a true story and that the directors were too embarrassed to make this story known to the public.

# Really? Again???

Have you ever felt like you have the worst luck ever? There's all kinds of ways to be unlucky. Maybe you miss the lottery jackpot by one number. Or perhaps you trip on stage right before your big break. The list of possible hard luck stories is endless. But those are only minor bad luck examples. What would you say to someone who's survived both the Hiroshima *and* Nagasaki Atomic bomb explosions from WWII? Yup. You'd call that person one of the unluckiest people ever. Or maybe the luckiest, because he survived BOTH!

Tsutomu Yamaguchi is actually one of the 260,000 people who survived the atomic bomb attacks, but he's among the very few who survived *both* attacks.

The day started like any other day. Yamaguchi was 29 at the time and on a business trip in Hiroshima. He was supposed to spend three months there and that fateful day, August 6, 1945, was actually to be his last day before he would head back home.

Yamaguchi worked for Mitsubishi Heavy Industries, and at about 8:15 that morning, he was on his way to Mitsubishi's shipyard. Suddenly, he heard something. He looked up and saw an American B-29 bomber sail through the skies overhead. It dropped what looked like a tiny thing with an equally tiny parachute. Moments later, the sky exploded. Yamaguchi said it looked like "the lightning of a huge magnesium flare." Without thinking, he jumped into a ditch to hide but the shock wave lifted him off the ground and threw him into a potato patch.

When he regained consciousness, he saw that his face and arms were burned badly, and his eardrums were ruptured. A mushroom cloud rose up over Hiroshima. He reached the Mitsubishi shipyard, and with two other survivors, spent the night at a raid shelter. The following day he caught a train to Nagasaki, passing through crowds of equally burned and confused people, and even swimming through a river of dead bodies.

He got home safely (or as safely as he could have) and immediately headed to the hospital. He learned that about 80,000 people died, and thousands more would die in the following weeks. They bandaged him up and sent him home to a family that barely recognized him. His own mother pointed her finger at him and called him a ghost.

Even though he was in bad shape, Yamaguchi went back to work just 3 days after surviving the Hiroshima explosion. His boss wanted a full report on it. Just as he was explaining what had happened, another blast was heard. Yamaguchi dropped to his knees as if he knew what was to come. Again.

Even though the second blast was stronger, the fact that the building he was in happened to be located on a hill and was well built, provided a better shelter this time. He was incredibly lucky, again being within two miles of an atomic explosion.

He immediately rushed home to check on his wife and child, who had taken refuge in a tunnel the moment they heard the explosion. His wife knew exactly what was happening because he had told her about his experience in Hiroshima. But unfortunately, all was not well. The following days found Yamaguchi sick with radiation poisoning. His hair fell out, he was vomiting, his burns wouldn't heal and would even turn gangrenous. But with time he recovered and was able to lead a normal life. As normal as someone who survived both Hiroshima and Nagasaki could, at least.

Until his death in 2009, he believed it was his destiny to survive the attacks and live to tell about it. He was recognized as a "nijyuu hibakusha," or "twice-bombed person."

# Revenge of the Tooth
# Without a Body

Sigurd Eysteinsson, also known as Earl Sigurd the Mighty, was a wise and powerful ruler who came to power purely by accident. His brother, Earl Rognvald of More, lost his son in war. The king wanted to compensate Rognvald somehow, and he figured he'd do it by offering him an earldom. Rognvald had other plans which included moving far, far away, so he just passed on the earldom to his brother, Sigurd.

Interestingly, there are more details known about Earl Sigurd's death than about his life. There was a feud between him and a guy named Maelbrigte. This guy had a funny nickname (as most nicknames are) and that was Maelbrigte Tusk. Why? He had this protruding tooth which you just couldn't miss.

Maelbrigte didn't like that Sigurd and his men had conquered a lot of Scottish territory, so the two men arranged to meet up for a duel, both of them bringing with them no more than 40 men. Despite the stain on his honor, Sigurd cheated. His excuse was that the Scots were not to be trusted, so he decided to double his odds. He brought 80 warriors, but he mounted them on only 40 horses. That was following the rules, right? Sigurd sure thought so.

At this point, Maelbrigte realized Sigurd was a cheat. Apparently, he saw from afar that there were two feet on each side of every horse. Maelbrigte's men lost, despite fighting bravely and proudly, but this is what usually happens when you're outnumbered.

It seemed that Sigurd wanted to add insult to injury, so he had his soldiers sever the heads of their dead enemies and then strap them all to their horses. Maelbrigte's head was reserved for his own saddle. Then they all rode back home, feeling victorious.

But Sigurd forgot one thing, and that is that even dead men can have their revenge on the living. And this is exactly what Maelbrigte somehow managed. Sigurd was spurring his horse during his ride home, and scratched his leg on Maelbrigte's big, weird tooth, the one he got his nickname for.

The result? A deadly infection which ended up costing Sigurd his life weeks later. It seems that Maelbrigte was the one who had the last laugh.

# Did You Notice My Pineapple?

People have always used symbols as a way to distinguish themselves from others. Today, people do it with cars, houses, golden jewelry, luxury watches, handbags, smartphones, and on and on. But what did they use as a status symbol in Great Britain during the 17th century? Well, a pineapple of course!

Boasting a whopping price of several thousand pounds, the pineapple of 17th century Britain was not for eating. Oh no. It would be paraded from one fancy mansion to the other, just laying there on the table during social gatherings, until it finally went rotten and it was no longer good for anything. It sounds ridiculous, but that is exactly what happened. You could even rent a pineapple for the evening, just so you could show it off a little and tuck it under your arm for a stroll, making sure everyone saw you with this prestigious status symbol.

Still, why would anyone consider a pineapple such a luxury? Well, in the 16th and the 17th century lots of exotic foods were imported from Europe and Asia. And somehow, the pineapple became the most coveted of them all. People generally connect ideas with fruit. For example, the apple has always been known as the forbidden fruit that tempted Eve in the Garden of Eden. And a pomegranate was responsible for keeping Persephone in the underworld half the year, according to the Greeks. The pineapple was free of any such notions so people could connect it to something completely new. Because of its exotic appearance and golden crown, it seemed like something royal.

Eventually, the Brits started growing it locally. You'd think this would take away from its exotic allure. But it didn't. In fact, only the very rich could grow it because of the financial investment. Pineapples require both heat and light, of which there wasn't enough in England's winter months. It required a lot of money to give this a try, without a guaranteed return. Plus, it took the fruit several years to bloom. So it was a tricky endeavor that only the wealthy could try.

All of these special characteristics made the pineapple extremely desired. People would even display it on special plates. The pineapple would be in the middle, just for show, never for actual eating. Placed around it would be an array of cheaper fruits. Guards were even hired to prevent thieves from stealing people's pineapples.

After years and years of the pineapple fad, steamships started importing them regularly and the prices dropped. Then everyone could afford them, even the working classes. And once something is available to the lower classes too, the aristocracy suddenly finds it no longer fashionable.

# I Think I've Been Here Before...

You know that feeling you sometimes have when it seems like something has happened before and all your hairs stand on end because you can't explain it? That's called deja vu. It's very unsettling and bizarre, which is why people have always found it so strange. There are lots of interesting theories that people have come up with over the years to try and explain this phenomenon.

The most common explanation is the "dual processing theory." When we notice something and acknowledge it, it goes straight into our short-term memory. If you don't make a conscious effort to memorize it, you'll forget it very quickly. A good example of short term memory would be cramming for a test the night before. You'll remember enough for the test, but if you don't regularly go over this subject matter, it will evaporate from your mind quickly, as if it never existed. Basically, this theory for explaining deja vu is that our brain is trying to store this new memory into long-term memory. This is where the feeling of "seen before" arises. Our brain just thinks we saw this thing before, when actually it's just moving the location of the memory.

Another scientific theory would be the "divided attention theory." In other words, your subconscious mind remembers the stimulus, but your conscious mind doesn't, and your brain is just playing around reorganizing stuff, such as messages you've received subconsciously, so that you feel them being familiar although you can't quite be sure about it.

One of the most interesting theories is the parallel universe theory. Some science fiction revolves around the premise that there are numerous parallel universes, which have thousands of versions of ourselves, all choosing a different possibility with a different outcome. The deja vu feeling then arises out of the idea that two parallel universes collide, meaning that while you're doing something here, another you in another parallel universe might be doing the very same thing, thus creating this feeling of unease. Crazy, right?!

Yet another interesting theory would be that deja vu is something like a sixth sense. You sense something would happen, as if you dream about it. This theory is actually backed up by some evidence. Research states that there were several people who had precognitive dreams about great disasters, such as the Titanic for example.

And finally, there's reincarnation. You know what the general idea is about. We die and are reborn to another life as something or someone else, with no knowledge of our previous lives. However, some people believe that there are some signals in this life which indicate some leftovers or reminders from our previous lives. Deja vu is seen as one of those signals, which is why it feels almost as if we're reliving some past moment, while in fact we can't really remember it.

Whatever it is, deja vu continues to baffle scientists while leaving us with that familiar feeling of something we've already experienced.

# Death by Dancing

I don't know about you, but I love dancing. It helps me get all the negative energy out of my system, just following the rhythm. Then when I'm all danced out, I stop. Imagine starting to dance, then when you want to stop...you can't. So you keep dancing and dancing, day and night, for weeks on end. Seems like some scary story. And yes, it is a scary story, but a scary true story. They called it the Dance Fever of 1518, when hundreds of people just started dancing and they couldn't stop for a whole month!

It started in mid-July in 1518 in a city called Strasbourg which is in modern day France. A woman basically went out into the street and she started dancing. Just like that. There wasn't even any music so she was dancing to some music only she could hear. Over the next week, she was joined by 100 more people, and they were all dancing together as if their lives depended on it.

Some genius came up with the idea that these people *needed* to keep dancing, otherwise they'd die. So a special place was set aside for the dancers. Music was provided. Even professional dancers were hired to cheer them on and keep them dancing.

Dancing is usually strenuous business. It gets you to sweat like crazy, especially if you've been dancing for over a week now, non-stop. This is when people with weaker hearts just started to drop down like flies. Dead. Within two weeks, there were 400 people dancing (despite the fact that people were dying).

Another clever idea came up, and that was to take all these dancers to a healing shrine. But around mid-September, the dancing stopped just as mysteriously as it had started. And the weirdest part? This wasn't even the first instance of crazy, non-stop dancing in history. It has happened ten times!

So what happened? The most popular theory suggests that all these people accidentally ingested something called ergot, a psychotropic mold that grows on stalks of the rye plant. Being on drugs makes one do crazy things, even dancing for weeks on end. But, they would also probably have experienced delusions and spasms. Plus, it usually cuts off blood supply to the extremities, which makes even walking hard, let alone dancing. So other theories have also been explored.

Another theory is also very plausible. The dancers were all members of the same cult, and someone powerful in the cult instructed them to dance. But there's a hole in this theory, too. Records say that the dancers were miserable and wanted to stop. They even begged the onlookers, with tears in their eyes, to stop their misery. So weird!

It seems then, that the most logical conclusion is that this dancing was the result of some mass hysteria. In 1518, the people of Strasbourg were very poor. People were dying of famine and disease, and they were hopeless about prospects for a better life. So it was easier to just believe that they were cursed, thinking that St. Vitus, a saint who had the power to take over their minds, forced them to dance until they were cleansed.

I guess at the time it just seemed easier to believe you were cursed and needed to dance your worries away.

# Robin Hood's Day Job

We all know the story of Robin Hood. He stole from the rich and selflessly gave to the poor, not keeping a single penny for himself. Ever since, people everywhere have always loved a good Robin Hood story.

As it turns out, Italy has a modern day Robin Hood by the name of Gilberto Baschiera. He was a bank manager, living a normal life in the small town of Forni di Sopra, which only has about 1000 people. But his normal life changed in a way he couldn't have predicted. Slowly but surely, he started taking small amounts of money from the bank accounts of rich clients who wouldn't even notice that the money was missing. Then he would transfer this money to the accounts of those who couldn't meet all the qualifications for credit. He did this for seven years until he was finally caught.

So how did it start? Baschiera was just a good guy who thought that bending the rules a little wouldn't harm anyone. That was how it all started. A local person came to the bank asking for a loan, but he didn't qualify. Baschiera felt bad for him, so he transferred the money from some rich client's account so that this other guy could qualify for a loan. More and more people would be granted loans this way, and most of them agreed to pay back the money. Baschieri, being the good guy that he was, believed them. He just forgot that not everyone does what they say they'll do. Of course some people just "forgot" to pay back the loan, which was how Baschiera was exposed.

When he was caught, he didn't lie. He admitted what he had done, and he explained why. He honestly thought he was helping people, and that they'd all eventually pay it back. The fact that he didn't benefit from this at all was the only thing that kept him out of prison. He even made sure to call every single person he had taken money from and explain his actions.

Since this was Baschiera's first offense and he didn't keep any of the money for himself, he was given only a two-year sentence, which he didn't even have to serve in jail.

While it seems that this story has a happy ending, it's not really so. Stealing is never okay. Not even when you're stealing for someone else who really needs that money. It's just not how things work. This is what Baschiera learned when in light of all the events, he lost both his job and his home.

Despite the fact that we all know stealing is wrong, we just can't seem to stay mad at a guy like Baschiera. He ended up taking over $1 million dollars and giving it to those he thought needed it more. But his Robin Hood days are likely over. He said, "But the price I paid is too high. I do not think I would do it again."

# The Shortest War in History Lasted for Less Than 45 Minutes

It started at 9:02 in the morning. The British didn't even have time for their morning tea. Not even an hour later, it was all finished. The British had won. And that's the story of the Anglo-Zanzibar war, also known as the shortest war in history. Short and sweet, right?

Just kidding. Even behind the shortest war there's a story to tell, which might even need more than 38 minutes, but I'll keep it short here.

It all started when the British Empire declared Zanzibar a protectorate of theirs. This meant that a new Sultan needed to be chosen, one who favored the British way of doing things. Meet Hamad bin Thuwaini, who stepped onto the stage in 1893.

All was fine and dandy for three years. Then he died. And by died, I mean that he was killed. On the very same day, his cousin Khalid bin Bargash barged into the palace and proclaimed himself the new Sultan. No foul play at all, right? Right. Moving on.

Needless to say, the Brits did not like this guy one bit. That's because he didn't want to dance to their tune. This is where Basil Cave, the British chief diplomat for Zanzibar, enters the story. He told Khalid to resign from the position he took without England's permission. Basil had also carefully positioned two

British warships (the HMS Philomel and the HMS Rush) close to the palace with their guns aimed straight at it. Soon, the HMS Sparrow joined in as the third musketeer.

Khalid got all nervous of course, trying to come up with a way out. The first thing he did was to hire more guards. He had about 3,000 men surrounding him. He also had a few artillery guns and a royal yacht which was no military ship, but it was armed.

Being all British and a stickler for rules, Basil Cave telegrammed the Foreign Office:

*Are we authorized in the event of all attempts at a peaceful solution proving useless, to fire on the Palace from the men-of-war?*

The following day, two more British warships joined in the party and Cave got his answer. It basically boiled down to *"adopt whatever measures you may consider necessary... do not, however, attempt to take any action which you are not certain of being able to accomplish successfully."* In other words, you may attack but only if you know you will win.

Finally, Cave ordered the Sultan to vacate the palace by 9 am the following morning. Hours passed by. No reply. Then at 8 am, the Sultan sent his reply:

*We have no intention of hauling down our flag and we do not believe you would open fire on us.*

The Sultan was right. Cave didn't want to open fire. So he sent one last message, wanting to be completely fair. Cave's message to the Sultan basically stated that he didn't want to open fire, but he would if provoked.

This is exactly how this shortest war in history started at exactly 9:02 am. Cave opened fire and as you might imagine, the heavy fire destroyed the walls of the palace. The Sultan's 3,000 guards were useless against battleships. Khalid immediately figured out that he couldn't win this war (surprise, surprise), so he slid out through the backdoor while his men bravely stood their ground.

By 9.40 am, it was obvious to Cave that he was merely beating a dead horse. No point wasting any more ammo, right? The fighting (well, fighting is a strong word for this) ceased. Cave's troops waltzed into the palace and brought down the flag of the Sultan, which signaled the end of the war. The official count? Exactly 44 minutes, no more, no less. Can you really call that a war?

About 500 of the Sultan's soldiers were wounded, some of them killed. There was only one British officer who got hurt. Apparently he dropped a teacup on his foot, spilling scorching hot tea. But he survived. Lucky guy.

A new Sultan was appointed, and there were no more revolutions in Zanzibar while it was under the British rule. As for Khalid, he was caught and then exiled to Saint Helena where he served some time, then returned home.

# A Teddy Bear Origin Story

We've all owned a teddy bear. Or two. Or five. It's just something no childhood should be without. We hugged them at bedtime, we dragged them by the little furry paw around the house, or even outside in the dirt, despite our mother's shouts that it would get filthy. We didn't care. We just wanted Teddy close to us. But do you know that our favorite bear got his name from an actual president? Yup. No less than President Theodore Roosevelt himself.

President Roosevelt was a hunting aficionado. He loved it. He lived for it. So one day, he was on a bear hunting trip in Mississippi. It was a chilly November day in 1902. But that didn't prevent either Roosevelt or his company from enjoying the hunt. It seemed though that the cold weather had sent the bears into hibernation earlier than usual, and there was not a single furry animal in sight.

At some point, Roosevelt separated from his company and shortly after, he heard them call out to him. He rushed over, and saw that his assistants cornered a black bear and tied it to a willow tree. The bear was helpless, growling at the hunters. His assistants urged Roosevelt to shoot the bear.

But Roosevelt took one look at the helpless bear and shook his head. He refused to do it. This wasn't why he went out hunting. He ordered them to release the bear, and they all returned home empty handed, thinking that was the end of things. It wasn't. The story somehow got published in the newspapers, and it reached people all around the country. Clifford Berryman, who was a political cartoonist working for the Washington Post, decided to use this story and make a little cartoon about what happened. People loved it.

But none more than Morris Michtom, who owned a candy shop in Brooklyn. In this shop, he and his wife would also make handmade stuffed animals, and seeing this cartoon gave them a great idea! They created a stuffed toy bear. They named it "Teddy's Bear," in honor of the president who wouldn't shoot a tied up animal.

They wrote to the president, asking to use his name and once they were given permission, they started producing the toy. As history shows, it was a huge success. Kids absolutely loved it and so did their parents, knowing the story behind it. This was how one man's refusal to shoot an animal led to the most famous toy in the world.

# Keep the Chocolate Train Going

Ah, Nutella. Those delectably delicious dollops of hazelnut chocolate cream. You can slather it on a piece of toast. You can cover your pancakes with it. Or perhaps the best way to enjoy it...just dip your spoon into the jar and stuff your face with it. Whatever your guilty pleasure is, Nutella has you covered.

But did you know that Nutella was just a very lucky result of someone trying to extend chocolate rations? Way back in 1806, Napoleon wanted to weaken British industry so he enforced an embargo on British goods. This meant that cocoa couldn't be imported, which sent chocolate prices sky high. All of Europe was affected by this but especially Italy, where people loved their chocolate.

However, the Piedmont region chocolatiers had a solution to this. In an effort to make the cocoa beans last longer and to make more products that still had chocolate, they just added hazelnuts to the chocolate. The result (which was totally amazing, by the way) was called *gianduja*. Even the name sounds delicious, right? This evened out the playing field but about 100 years later, during WWII, the same thing happened. Chocolate became super expensive once more, reserved only for the well off. But let's face it. Everyone likes chocolate, whether they're rich or poor.

This is when pastry maker Pietro Ferrero solved this confectionery crisis in the same manner as had been done a century ago. He added his hometown's famous hazelnuts to his chocolate and called the brand, Pasta Gianduja. At first it was just a solid block of hazelnut chocolate paste. But it was still delicious and it sold like crazy. Then, five years later in 1951, he made a creamy version of it. He called it Supercrema. Michele, Pietro's son, dabbled a little with the original recipe and voila! Supercrema became Nutella in 1964.

This Nutella, the one we all know and love, made Michele Ferrero a very rich man. In fact, his son who inherited his chocolate company, is now the richest man in Italy with a worth of $35 billion. Not bad for a chocolatier, right?

# Don't Die Here

Svalbard, a remote Norwegian island, and the town of Longyearbyen are an Arctic wonderland for those who enjoy snow and cold. There is actually no place you can live on Earth that is further north. There is a lot of darkness in the winter, almost four whole months of absolutely no distinction between night and day. That's fine if you're a night bird, but for those who actually thrive on sunlight... good luck. And the polar bears aren't very friendly at all if you have the misfortune of stumbling upon one. However, this still isn't the weirdest thing to watch out for in Svalbard. There's about 3,000 island residents there and they all abide by one rule. Whatever you do, you can't die in Svalbard.

I hear you asking, what? But it's true. They've made it illegal to die in Svalbard because it's so cold there. All this started in the 1950s, when some of the locals discovered something strange (although under the circumstances, I guess it wasn't so strange, just cold). The buried bodies weren't decomposing because it was so insanely cold.

You may think, so what? Maybe the bodies just took more time to decompose, but there was no way that absolutely nothing was happening to them, all buried and stuff, right? Wrong. Get this. In 1998, scientists exhumed corpses of the people who died of the flu pandemic in 1918. That's 80 years worth of decomposition. The bodies were so well preserved that live samples of the deadly virus could still be extracted from the bodies!

Dead bodies spread disease even more quickly and efficiently than live ones. So the locals got scared of this and figured out that they simply wouldn't be burying any more people in the local cemetery. Sounds simple, right?

Well, not really. What do you do with dead bodies if you can't bury them? You forbid living people from dying there, of course! This means that anyone who is at a risk of dying is sent to the mainland. For example, terminally ill people must leave the island. There is actually a small hospital in Svalbard, but even pregnant women are advised to fly to the Norwegian mainland and give birth there. Just in case.

So while it isn't actually a law, (because how would you punish those who break it?), dying on the island is heavily discouraged. If a person does unexpectedly die on the island, burial in coffins are prohibited so the bodies are cremated.

# Where Is His Mind?

If there's anyone's brain we'd like to pick, then it's definitely Einstein's. Thomas Harvey, the pathologist who was on call when Einstein died on April 18, 1955, actually got to do that. How? He stole Einstein's brain.

Before his death, Einstein left specific instructions on his burial. He wanted to be cremated, and then have his ashes scattered secretly somewhere, just so fans wouldn't make his grave into a big deal. Or even worse, so that his brain and body wouldn't be dissected and studied. Unfortunately, that's exactly what happened.

Even though neither Einstein nor his family wanted to have his brain studied, Harvey, being a pathologist with access to the dead body, stole the brain. He then pressured Einstein's family into actually allowing him to continue with his scientific investigation on the brain.

Harvey lost his job when the administration at Princeton hospital (where Einstein had died) heard what happened. But Harvey kept the brain, and took it with him to Philadelphia. But he didn't keep it in one piece. He cut it up into 240 pieces, and had them all preserved. All 240 pieces fit into two jars. Where did he keep these two jars? Where you keep all suspicious and dark stuff you don't want others to know about... the basement!

But this is not where the story ends. This is where it actually gets even stranger! Harvey's wife didn't like the idea of a brain in her basement (even if it was Einstein's), so she told Harvey to get rid of it. Harvey cleverly hid the brain in a cider box under his cooler. Eventually, Harvey moved to Missouri where he tried to practice medicine but lost his license when he couldn't pass a three-day competency exam. All the while, he kept studying Einstein's brain.

He mostly kept it a secret, but on occasion he would tell people he had Einstein's brain and he could even share a piece of it. Some believed him, others thought it was just a bad joke.

In 1985, he worked with some people on the first study of Einstein's brain. The results showed significant differences in individual cells and even structures. But it was all to be taken with a grain of salt. I mean, seriously. The brain was kept in jars and coolers! There's no way that the results could be accurate, seeing as how so much time had passed and the brain wasn't stored properly by a guy who lost his medical license.

It seems that even Einstein knew that this would all be a fool's errand. That's probably why he specifically stated that he didn't want his brain to be studied. Even beyond the grave, the man proves to be a genius.

# The Royal Truck Mechanic

When you think of the British Queen, many things come to mind. Royalty. Old age (she's become the longest reigning queen). Big castle. But, you might never think the word "truck mechanic" could be possibly related to her. And you'd be wrong.

When WWII started in 1939, Elizabeth was only 13 years old. Her sister Margaret was even younger. She was 9. So naturally, the Queen Mother was urged by those closest to her to evacuate with her family to Canada. She outright refused to do so. They spent most of the war in Buckingham Palace, but because it was bombed on numerous occasions, they kept changing their location. They finally chose Windsor Castle as their permanent residence.

In February of 1945, the war was going full blast. Elizabeth, who had then turned 18, didn't want to sit on the sidelines but rather wanted to be actively involved in the fight. Her father wouldn't hear of it at first. But she eventually managed to persuade him. Her training began in March 1945, and she became an honorary second subaltern in the Auxiliary Territorial Service. Basically, she was a second lieutenant. Even as a member of the royal family, she wasn't given any special perks and she worked hard to prove herself. As such, she was the first woman in the royal family who became "a full-time active member in the women's service." Today she is still the only woman in the royal family who ever served in the military.

As a member of the Auxiliary Territorial Service, Elizabeth learned her way around taking care of the military vehicles in use. She wasn't afraid of getting down and dirty while refueling, making sure that the oil and fluids were topped, taking care of tire pressure, etc. She learned how to change tires and rebuild engines. Women of the ATS were responsible for making batteries and locating enemy aircraft.

By the end of the war, the future queen had worked her way through the ranks and had been given the title of junior commander in the ATS. She even became a fully certified driver of military vehicles. A magazine article published in 1947 said of the future queen, "One of her major joys was to get dirt under her nails and grease stains in her hands, and display these signs of labor to her friends."

The role of women in the military during this time was not without risk. Even though they were not on the front lines of combat, occasionally vehicles driven by the women mechanics would be bombed. The women had to use caution and practice safety while doing their military duties.

When World War 2 ended on May 8th, Victory in Europe Day, Elizabeth quietly left Buckingham palace and celebrated with the commoners. She and her sister Margaret, along with a few sneaky guards, took to the streets to party with the happy crowds.

Elizabeth wore her ATS military uniform so she would better blend in with the others. Even before she was the queen, Elizabeth was showing her pride and dedication to her country.

# Now Don't Move for 8 Hours

We live in a world where taking a photograph is literally as easy as pressing a button. About 1.8 billion photographs are shared daily! That's a whole lotta frozen moments in time. But how does this work? What magic do cameras use to freeze a moment in time?

It's all about light. If you're standing in a room that has no source of light, you wouldn't see much, right? You wouldn't see anything really. Just darkness. But if you have something as small as a flashlight, things change. You can see. Pay attention to that flashlight (try to imagine it in your mind). How does the light move? In a straight line, right? Then when it hits an object, the light bounces off of it and you see what's in front of you.

Light is constantly bouncing off of stuff, and it's going in all directions. The first camera ever created was a whole room which had a hole in one wall. Light would go inside though that hole, in a straight line, aiming straight for the opposite wall. It was like watching a projection of something. Then someone came up with a great idea. Place material that is sensitive to light at the back of that room. Boom! You've got the first photography studio.

The guy who thought of it was an Arab physicist by the name of Ibn Al-Haytham. He created what is known today as camera obscura. Of course, it's much different from the cameras we have today, but he was off to a great start. Also, he didn't create it to take pictures but to project light. Photography came later.

In 1827, a French scientist named Joseph Nicephore Niepce took the first photo with a camera obscura. He put an engraving onto a metal plate, which was coated in bitumen (a black tarry substance you can find in cement). Then he exposed it to light. The dark areas on the engraving made sure the light couldn't pass through, but the areas which weren't coated in it allowed the light to react with the chemicals. Slowly, the first photographs appeared!

While the idea was awesome, the down side was that it required about 8 hours of light exposure. Can you imagine holding your pose that long? I can't either. Plus, if you held your pose for 8 hours and then the image didn't turn out...you'd be pretty upset. Only later did Louis Daguerre improve the process, bringing it down to less than 30 minutes, and there was no risk of the image disappearing. His process was called the daguerreotype. By 1850, there were daguerreotype studios all over the world. In New York City there were as many as 70.

Next time you take a photo, just remember to be grateful that it's so easy to take 50 photos in just a flash, keeping only that perfect Instagram-worthy one. You could have been stuck sitting in one pose for 8 hours.

# Land of the Flying Rhinos

Is it a bird? Is it a plane? No? It's upside down rhinos!

And no, Superman isn't helping transport them. Regular old helicopters are. If you're asking yourself what rhinos are doing flying upside down in the skies above Namibia, then you're in the right place. I've been asking myself that very same question. And the answer is so simple you'll be amazed.

One third of the world's rhinoceros population lives in Namibia. Only, they can't just live anywhere they'd like. People who are responsible for conserving their species need to relocate them strategically so that different rhinos can breed, thus providing for the much needed genetic diversity.

Also, there are lots of poachers who keep hunting down these beautiful animals for their precious horns. This means that conservationists need to relocate the rhinos to national parks or other kinds of reservations to help the rhino population continue to grow.

Now imagine. You need to move rhinos. Not one rhino, but several probably. And they're huge. Humongous. They weigh between 4,000 and 5,000 pounds. It's not like you can just ask them nicely to go somewhere, right? Nope. You have to physically move them.

Namibia is pretty rough. There are savannas, salt flats and sand dunes. So even if you could get your jeep close to the rhinos (many times that's not even an option), try coming up with a way to get the rhino to actually go into the vehicle. To me, the whole thing sounds like mission impossible. If somehow by sheer luck, you could get it to go inside, the journey lasts hours. No rhino is going to enjoy that. Who would?

So these guys thought long and hard about what the best way to transport rhinos would be. Then...a light bulb. You take a rhino. You sedate it. You tie it up by its feet. You blindfold it. Then you lift it up in the air, hanging upside down. Bingo!

I know you might think this just sounds crazy (and you'd be kinda right), but hear me out. Zoologists know that when you give sedatives to an animal (or to a human, it works on us too), positioning is crucial. If not positioned properly, the rhino's chest and lungs could be compressed, making breathing difficult. And we all know what happens if we can't breathe for whatever reason.

They tried lying the rhino down on its side instead of lying upside down, to check heart and breathing functions. Lying upside down, the rhino could actually breathe better. Why? Zoologists think it's because the rhino's head and neck are hanging down, so the airways are open, allowing for free flow of air.

A sedated rhino is also a very quiet rhino. Blindfolding also helps because most animals that can't see will become more calm. So a combination of many things assist the zoologists in being able to help the rhinos and give them the best shot at continuing to populate and thrive.

And this my friends...is why Namibia is the land of flying, upside down rhinos.

# A World Without Ketchup?

None of us can imagine a barbecue, or even eating a quick hot dog without ketchup. In fact, about 97% of homes in the US own a bottle at any given point of the week. But have you ever wondered about the history of this wonderful condiment which makes french fries so delicious?

First of all, you need to know that when it first appeared it wasn't even made of tomatoes! It was actually made of fish guts, meat byproducts and soybeans. Yum. The name comes from "ge-thcup" or "koe-che-up" which is what the people speaking the Southern Min dialect of China used to call this sauce. They loved it because they could take it with them on long overseas trips, without fear that it would spoil.

Eventually, in the early 1700s, the British traders who traveled to Indonesia and the Philippines decided to try it. They liked it so much that they brought it home and dabbled a bit with the recipe. That's not to say they completely changed it. What followed was the golden era of ketchup. It appeared in all the cookbooks, and you could make it out of anything really. This included, but wasn't limited to oysters (Oyster ketchup? Really?), mussels, mushrooms, celery, plums, you name it. What they did was basically boil some piece of fruit or vegetable (or sea creature!) or mix it with salt and leave it like that for an extended period of time. The end product? A pleasantly tangy, salty, and very flavorful spread which would last for quite awhile. And in a time where you didn't have the commodity of a refrigerator, it was handy to have foods that wouldn't spoil.

1812 was when the ketchup we all know and love was created. You know, the tomato kind. The guy who invented it was named James Mease, and he used "love apples" to make it (that's what they used to call tomatoes back then). Before the time of vinegar, it was tough to preserve sauces made with tomatoes, because they'd go bad very quickly. This is where Heinz stepped in. They mixed tomatoes, salt, spices, brown sugar, and... distilled vinegar. They put it into a glass bottle and voila! The birth of the first Heinz ketchup took place in 1876.

Somewhere between the birth of tomato-y ketchup and the Heinz bottle, Dr. John Cooke Bennet thought it was a good idea to sell ketchup as medicine. People knew that fruits and vegetables contained valuable vitamins, so Bennet advertised tomato ketchup as a concoction which could cure anything from diarrhea and indigestion, to rheumatism and even jaundice. He even sold it in pill form. But by 1850, people figured out it doesn't really do anything, apart from taste delicious.

Today, you can't imagine a household without ketchup. And many people prefer Heinz. A whopping 650 million bottles are sold every single year. But the real deal, not the oyster ketchup. Thanks, but I'll definitely pass on that.

# Don't Fear Falling From the Sky?

Flying has become something that happens every day, just like riding in a car. You don't even think about it. Especially if you want to travel to visit other continents and countries, flying is basically your only option. But many people still suffer from aviophobia, which is the fear of flying. Some suffer just mild symptoms such as nerves and general discomfort, but they still manage to get on the plane and travel. Others with more severe cases, can't even board a plane without thinking it's bound to crash and kill everyone onboard. So how do you fight this phobia? You could start by learning more about plane safety and statistics.

Rest assured, people who fly planes tend to be pretty good at what they do. They're pretty great, actually. There's a rigorous training program to get certified to fly airplanes. Then pilots need to do thousands of practice flight hours before they are allowed to fly commercial planes. Also, pilots go through constant training and recertification at all points in their careers.

The Federal Aviation Administration says that there are about 40,000 flights with as many as 2.6 million passengers flying every single day. And that's in the United States alone! Other statistics between 2012 and 2016 would include the following:

- 98.6% of crashes didn't result in a single fatality
- The chance of dying in a plane crash would be 1 in 3.37 billion

In 2017, there were actually no major passenger plane crashes anywhere in the world, making it the safest year to fly, although there were even more flights taking off than the year before. But the most important piece of info is that according to the National Transportation Safety Board, 95 percent of passengers that are actually involved in aviation accidents survive. Taking into account accidents between 1983 and 2000, which involved more than 53,000 passengers, the results showed that 51,207 people made it out alive. Those are pretty good odds, considering it's a seventeen year span!

It could have been that they were lucky, but maybe they knew a few tips to increase the chances of survival. What are those? First, get ready for impact. Lower your torso. This helps you avoid hitting the seat in front of you. Then make sure to hold your legs and keep your feet on the floor. This might save you from a broken or sprained ankle. After surviving a plane crash, you'd want to be able to keep moving. Next, try to find something to protect your head. You could, for example, cushion your headrest with a pillow or your coat. Make sure to keep your seatbelt on at all times. You'd be surprised how many people forget this. Last but not least, stay calm. Panic only makes your reactions slower, and in an accident...

even a single second could mean the difference between life and death.

But sometimes we're just asking for it. Like the time in Italy in 2009 when a new bride wanted something special at her wedding. She hired a pilot to toss the bouquet down to the wedding party. But unluckily, the bouquet went right into the engine causing it to explode. Thankfully, neither the pilot or any of the wedding party were injured at all. No word on if the pilot went back to the wedding party for a few dances.

Whether you're flying over weddings or not, don't forget to enjoy the flight! Keep all of this in mind and hopefully the next time you have the opportunity to board an airplane, you will feel safe knowing you are in great hands. The pilots have been well trained and the odds really ARE in your favor. Happy travels!

# Typhoid Fever for You, and You, and You

In the 1900s, typhoid fever was known to affect mostly the poor, because of their lack of hygiene and horrible sanitation practices. So how come there was an outbreak in Long Island, where rich New Yorkers would spend their lazy summers? In the words of a smart detective, the cook did it.

The cook's name was Mary Mallon. She was even born in Cookstown, Ireland in 1869 and she immigrated to the US when she was just 15. She stayed with her aunt and uncle there. As was the custom for poor immigrant women, she got a job as a cook. She had quite a knack for it and it paid much better than other domestic positions.

It was the hot summer of 1906, and Mary was hired by Charles Henry Warren. His family rented a summer house in Oyster Bay, Long Island and they needed a cook. Just weeks later, the Warrens' daughter got ill. The diagnosis, typhoid fever. Soon, the rest of the household started dropping like flies. Quickly the madam of the house, the two maids, the gardener, and then another daughter got sick. Half of the household had the fever.

Seeing that the Warrens rented the place and then got sick, the owners were worried that they wouldn't be able to rent the place again unless they found the source of the contagion. So they hired George Soper. He was a civil engineer, who had some experience with typhoid outbreaks. In other words, he knew what he was doing and immediately, the shadow of doubt fell on the cook.

You see, Mary had a strategy. Whenever a typhoid fever outbreak would appear in a household she was working, she would leave a week or two after. This was what happened at the Warren house as well. Soper knew that the outbreak could have been caused only by food or someone handling it. So he traced Mary's employment history, and what do you know? Typhoid outbreaks happened in every single household she worked! There were 7 households and 22 people got sick. Some sources state that the numbers are even higher, but these are the numbers that are known for sure.

Of course, this was more than just coincidence. But he couldn't just point his finger at Mary and say, it was you, you did it. He had to do it the scientific way which meant asking her a question no lady should ever be asked. Madam, could you spare a stool and urine sample, please?

Despite knowing that this would be a rather un-pleasant conversation, Soper knew it had to be done. So he went to Mary's newest place of work, and just told her what he needed. This was what he said: "I had my first talk with Mary in the kitchen of this house...I was as diplomatic as possible, but I had to say

I suspected her of making people sick and that I wanted specimens of her urine, feces and blood." Pretty straightforward, right?

Only, Mary didn't take too kindly to this. Apparently, she grabbed a fork and went after him. He rushed out of the kitchen, deciding to leave the conversation for another time. Maybe when she was in a better, less violent mood. The second time he tried asking her for her stool, urine, and blood sample, Mary ran. They spent 5 hours looking for her, then found her hiding in a closet. They brought her out, kicking and screaming.

As you'd expect, they found the typhoid bacilli in her stool. They brought her to an isolated cottage on North Brother Island. They kept her there for several years, against her will. The question everyone was wondering was, "Can the government really do this? Hold someone against their will like that? I mean, she hasn't broken any laws." It was generally believed that she didn't know she carried the bacteria, and that sick people always showed symptoms. She had none.

The health officials still claimed that anybody who was dangerous and sick needed to be separated from everyone else. And health officials could quarantine any person they thought contagious. Mary, of course, believed she was innocent.

She was isolated for 2 years, and every week she gave stool samples. Out of 163 samples, 120 were positive. Apparently, she also sent samples to a private lab and they came back negative. She was furious, demanding

to be set free. Then in 1910, a new health commission-
er came onboard and he took pity on Mary. He told
her she could go free if she never worked as a cook
again. What do you think happened?

Mary agreed, of course. She would never again
work as a cook and she would take all hygienic precau-
tions to protect others from infection. Unfortunately...
she lied. She still didn't believe she was sick, but that
it was all some conspiracy against her. So after some
short time of being a laundress, she went back to being
a cook. About 5 years after her release, there was a typhoid fever outbreak in the Sloane Maternity Hospital in Manhattan. As many as 25 got sick, and 2 died.
The culprit? Mary Mallon.

The public wanted to burn her at the stake. The
first time was a coincidence. But this time? No way.
She put all those people at risk on purpose. So the
only way they could keep others safe was to isolate her.
They sent her back to North Brother Island and that
was where she remained for 23 years, until she died.

In a way, one can't help but feel pity for her being
treated that way. Then again, all she had to do was stop
cooking for other people. How hard could that have
been?

# I got Shotgun!

Riding shotgun in the front passenger seat of the car is the best. You don't have the responsibility of watching the road like the driver does but you still get to enjoy the view in front. It's much better than sitting in the back, which usually has less legroom and not as good of a view. It's a wonderful day when you're finally old enough to ride up in the front seat of your parent's car. But there are several rules to follow when calling shotgun. Do you know them?

First, you shout shotgun as loud as you can. Duh. But you have to be by the car, just about to get into it. It doesn't work if you're shouting it from a mile away. Also, it doesn't count unless someone's there to hear you call it. Finally, it's only valid for one ride. You can't call out shotgun and make it last for all rides. While today this is a game for us, it was quite the responsibility to occupy this seat back in the days of the wild frontier. And dangerous.

The term "ride shotgun" originated in the 1880s, when stagecoaches were used to transport all kinds of valuables, including money. They would often be employed by financial institutions such as banks. And banks wanted to make sure that the valuables they were sending would reach their destination safe and sound. For this, a shotgun messenger would be added to the trip.

So on these trips, you'd have both the stagecoach driver and the guy watching out for him. This guy would usually be armed with a shotgun, just in case some local desperados tried to rob them. Needless to say, these two men were given strict orders to protect their cargo at all cost. And if the journey was very long, it was easier to have two people along for the ride so they could alternate driving and sleeping.

The 1880's was the height of the Wild West. Tombstone, Arizona was one of the key places in the history of the West. The famous marshall, Wyatt Earp, made it out to Tombstone in 1879 and worked as a stagecoach shotgun hand until he was appointed Deputy Sheriff two years later.

One story of a shotgun rider involves Bob Paul, who was a lawman and friend of Wyatt Earp. One night in 1881, Bob was on a stagecoach with $26,000 in silver aboard. He was traveling from Tombstone to a train station so the silver could get back East. That silver would be worth nearly $700,000 today. No wonder they had to be careful! The guy who usually drove wasn't feeling well so he handed the reins over to Bob and took the shotgun seat so he could rest.

Suddenly an outlaw stepped out into the road and told Bob to come to a stop. Two of his companions then came out with guns drawn. Quickly Bob unloaded his gun at the cowboys, wounding one. Bob was unscathed but the usual driver wasn't so lucky. He had taken a bullet to the chest and was killed. Bob always thought about how that bullet would have been his if he had been in his usual seat. The horses were spooked by all the shooting and it took Bob nearly a mile to get control of them again. That's how it was for stagecoach shotgun hands in those days.

Of course, we don't ride around in the front seat carrying shotguns any longer and let's hope we keep it that way! But it's fun to discover this slang phrase's origin.

# The Man Who Saved Over 400 People from Jumping Off a Bridge

The Yangtze River Bridge in Nanjing, China has the highest rate of suicides of any other place in the world. People who are feeling like they have no hope left, head to this bridge to end their suffering. If they are lucky, they will meet Chen Si before their fate is sealed.

Chen Si has become known as a guardian angel here on earth. It all started in 2003. Chen had a vegetable stand in downtown Nanjing. He was having trouble making enough money to support his family. He went for a walk to clear his head and ended up on the Yangtze Bridge where he saw a man who had climbed over the railing and was preparing to jump into the turbulent waters below. Chen grabbed the man, pulling him over the railing and tackling him to the ground, thus saving the man's life.

After that, Chen Si took it upon himself to help patrol the bridge, looking for people who seemed desperate and hopeless. He stops them, sometimes having to get physically involved, literally pulling them back to the safe side of the railing. What does he do after that? He talks to them, listens to them, and sometimes even takes them back to the apartment that he rented so he could live close to the bridge.

Chen gives these people what they needed all along. He listens and helps. In one case, a man was considering suicide because he owed so much money for his daughter's leukemia treatment. Chen helped him by calling the hospitals about a payment plan. He called the man every week to check on him.

"I just want to bring light to those who are in the dark," Chen says. And his mission is clearly needed as Chen has saved 412 people! He writes their names down in a diary to help him remember.

Still, Chen doesn't consider himself a hero. He grew up in a poor family and knows the struggles that many people are facing. He does this because he is interested in people and in helping. Chen has inspired others to help patrol the bridge as well. He has volunteers, including a few psychology students from local universities whom he has trained in spotting and helping those who seem to be troubled.

"There is a saying in China," he says, "the prosperity of a nation is everyone's responsibility. How can we all avoid this responsibility?"

Thankfully for so many people, Chen Si is a citizen who doesn't shy away from the responsibility of caring. He gives hope and connection to so many in need. He is truly the Nanjing Angel.

# 200,000 Tons of Bombs, Quietly Lurking

Even though WWII ended a long time ago, there are still leftover bombs in German cities being excavated. What happens when they are found? Well, people are alerted, traffic is rerouted, areas get evacuated, and everyone gets just a little bit nervous. We're talking about bombs after all.

It is estimated that between 1940 and 1945, Allied Forces dropped somewhere around 2.7 million tons of explosive objects. They ranged anywhere from small incendiary charges which were supposed to set wooden buildings on fire, to bombs weighing several tons. About 1 in every 5 dropped bombs didn't explode. That means there were about 250,000 duds. Usually, the dropped bombs would get buried several feet into the ground and just stay there. Years later, they would begin to be unearthed.

Cities in Western Germany like Cologne, Düsseldorf, and Bremen, were under heavy fire and it's a common thing for bombs to be found there. In Berlin, two thousand live bombs have been discovered since the war. Some say there are still 15,000 hiding under the city. People are basically walking on ticking time bombs. Scary, right?

It sure was for Paule Dietrich. On October 7, 2013, city workers for the city of Oranienburg, Germany showed up at his house. Paule thought it was some friends coming to help celebrate his birthday. But that was not the case. The workers declared that his yard was *ein verdachtspunkt*, or "a point of suspicion." How's that for a birthday present?

For about six weeks, workers located and studied a 1000 pound bomb that was buried 12 feet below ground, right next to Paule's house. 1000 pounds! That's a big bomb. On November 19th, the head of the investigation told Paule he needed to evacuate his home. Nearby streets and houses were also evacuated and trains were shut down. The bomb could not be defused and so it had to be detonated. Paule was taking his dog for a walk in a nearby forest when he heard the explosion. BOOM!

When Paule was able to return home, he found a crater 60 feet across, filled with debris. His front porch was leaning precariously into the crater. Still, Paule said that he feels like his family was lucky. Every summer his grandchildren visited, playing in a plastic pool and camping directly over top of where the bomb was buried.

In the future, Paule hopes to build another house on the property, but he is not in a hurry to get started. Workers have found two more possible bombs on Paule's land.

Most of the time, when a bomb is found it can be defused so that it doesn't explode and cause so much destruction. In such cases, the police will still evacuate the area for safety. Many of these bombs are so hidden, experts on bomb removal say that it is likely that they will still be finding bombs 200 years from now!

# "Stop! Police Geese! Honk!"

Who do you think are the best guard animals in the world? Dogs, right? Well, Chinese policemen beg to differ. They have geese, and they say they're never going back to dogs.

You'd never connect geese to police work or any kind of guard duty would you? But you'd be surprised. Their ability to create a ruckus is unparalleled. And unlike our canine friends who are all too easily bought with a good chunk of meat, geese will not sell you out for a treat. On the contrary. The more you try to bribe them, the louder they will honk, waking up the entire block.

Geese also have great eyesight. They've got an extra light sensor, which allows them to see further and in much greater detail than us humans. Best of all, they are super territorial and vigilant, especially at night. If they sense any kind of alarm, one will start honking and the rest will follow suit.

Duan Wencheng, leader of one of the police stations, said that their skills shouldn't be doubted and those who did were made to swallow their own words when their geese prevented a theft. One summer, a farmer was caught by the police riding an unlicensed motorbike. When he was stopped he fled on foot and the police were left with his motorbike, which they brought back to the station. The farmer thought he'd just sneak into the police station and get his bike back. Sounds like a simple plan. Only it was foiled by geese.

The farmer killed the guard dog by giving it poisoned meat but he wasn't counting on the goose squad. They began honking aggressively, spreading their wings and flapping them menacingly. He knew better than to mess with them. Eventually he got caught, all thanks to the geese.

Not only that, but the geese can recognize police uniforms, so they know never to attack an officer. In the rural police stations of China, the geese are just part of the team.

# How Could A Mom Fail 4 DNA Tests?

Every single cell in your body contains DNA. It's what makes you...you. It's a long molecule that reveals your genetic code, your marker, your unique identity. It is passed down genetically, which means we inherit the same DNA from our parents in a fifty fifty ratio. So it's one of the most sure ways to prove that someone is related. Unless you're Lydia Fairchild, that is, who thought that applying for public assistance would be a piece of cake. But a DNA test showed that she wasn't the mother of her own 3 children. The same 3 kids she carried in her womb and gave birth to!

So what happened? And how did it happen?

Lydia was 26 at the time and unemployed, so she went and applied for public assistance in Washington state. It all seemed like such an easy process. The whole family just had to do a simple test to prove they were all related. When you know you carried and gave birth to those kids, there's not a shadow of doubt in your mind.

Well, it turns out it's not always that simple. Lydia received a call to come in at once and meet with the representative of the department of Social Services. She thought it was just standard procedure. Nothing to worry about. Then the meeting turned into one of those cop scenes from the movies where the police are interrogating the suspect, forcing them to confess a crime they didn't commit.

Lydia's crime? Not being the mother of her own children!

*Who are you? Whose children are those?* Questions like these came at Lydia, who was in complete shock. She remained calm, saying it must all be just a mistake. Someone mixed up the test results. They must have, right? Then a social worker said, "No. DNA is 100% foolproof and it doesn't lie."

Lydia found herself in a nightmare. Needless to say, she was denied government assistance. Not only that, she was also suspected of kidnapping her babies! They could come and take her kids at any moment. She couldn't believe it.

When she got home, she found her old photos of when she was pregnant. When she told her parents what happened, they couldn't believe it either. Especially not her mother who was there and saw the kids being born! The whole thing was crazy. Lydia got in touch with her doctor for all the births. He was on her side. He was sure that the kids were hers and he also wondered what could have gone wrong with the tests that are usually infallible.

New tests were issued. Different lab, same results. According to the DNA, the kids weren't Lydia's. She had to get a lawyer and go to court to prove that the kids were hers so she could keep them. Frightening, isn't it?

Finding a lawyer proved to be another obstacle. No lawyer wanted to go against DNA results. Finally, she found someone willing to take the chance. Alan Tindell agreed to help but questioned her about everything. Her answers were always the same and eventually, he believed her.

Suddenly there was a break! Another woman across the country had the same problem. Karen Keegan's DNA also didn't match any of her children's. After trying everything, Karen finally remembered that she had a thyroid nodule removed. A sample of it was saved, and the DNA from that matched her sons.

So what does this mean? Her thyroid was the only organ in her body that had the same DNA as her children. Cue dramatic music...Karen was her own twin! What???
Basically, her blood has one DNA but some other body parts have another. How? There were two fertilized eggs in Karen's mom's womb that would have developed into twins. Only instead of developing, they merged. This resulted in two distinct genetic codes. Two different DNA's. This is called chimerism. It's from Greek mythology *chimera,* meaning a monster who was part lion, part snake, and part goat.

After a while it was proved that Lydia was also her own twin. Luckily her story also had a happy ending despite the infallible DNA results that tried to prove that she wasn't her kids' mother.

# You'll Pry My Teacup From
# My Cold Dead Hands

What do the British love the most? Their Queen, fish and chips, dry humor, and of course...tea. Tea is quite possibly the first thing that pops to your mind when you think of the British. It is no wonder then that ever since WWII when the British Centurion main battle tank appeared, all British tanks and armored fighting vehicles have been fully equipped with tea making facilities.

While you may think it's a joke, the British never joke about tea. Be it war or peace, they like to partake in their daily tea. So they found a way to make tankers fit teatime into their fighting schedule. After all, isn't that what gentlemen do?

The British tanks come with a little thing called a boiling vessel, which can be used for many things, including brewing some nice tea when the tanker is not on war duty. All joking aside, the boiling vessel wasn't created *specifically* for the British to be able to enjoy their cup of tea during war...although they added this nice perk to the general list of possibilities.

This boiling vessel isn't a kettle. It's more of an electric thermos which has the ability to heat up anything you put inside such as water, soups, any kinds of rations, coffee, etc. And the best part? It's small so it doesn't get in the way of the tank's functioning in any way and is neatly tucked in the back.

So basically, any time the brave British gents felt like having a good old spot of tea on the front, all they had to do was pour in some hot water and select their favorite tea. There you go. Afternoon tea at five won't be missed, even if fighting on the front lines.

You may think that soldiers being inside their tanks all the time was bad, but it was actually beneficial for them. While they were inside, they were much safer. Even in the worst case scenario, they were safer inside the tank than outside because the tank is sealed off from the rest of the world. Some reports state that 37% of all tanker casualties during World War II happened with men outside the tank, not in it.

So having this neat little boiling vessel inside the tank all safely nestled in the back, helped keep the men safe and unharmed. But best of all, it had a little reminder of home.

# What's for Dessert?

Would you like to try your hand at a Danish tongue twister? A tongue twister that has even helped to protect borders during times of war? One that's so tricky, you don't even need to make it a whole sentence? It's just a phrase. *Rødgrød med fløde.* One thing's for sure... if you can pronounce this the right way, congrats.

To settle the mystery, rødgrød med fløde is actually a dessert. It's red porridge with cream, to be exact. Apart from being horribly difficult to pronounce, it's delectably delicious. It's a vividly colored compote of red fruits (which is where the rødgrød comes from), that has been cooked and thickened into a compote. It's topped with some whipped cream (the fløde part). It's the Danish dessert recipe that has withstood the test of time. You simply must try it if you ever get the chance to visit Denmark.

So back to the tongue-twisting dessert name. There's the three Øs (whatever that sound is!), then two rather guttural Danish Rs (okay, we might be able to do this if we really, really, really try), and then you slide in four soft Ds (compared to the Øs, this should be the easy part). The Danish r is guttural, while the English r is pronounced in the front of the mouth. This means the Danish r is more of a hr sound. Roughly, the right pronunciation of the phrase would be this one: *hrooth ghrooth mith floothuh.* Did you get that?

The English would just say "roygroy ma flyrr." And they'd be totally wrong. And back in the days of WWII, they would be dead wrong. You see, the phrase is so hard to pronounce that it's nearly impossible for foreigners. Everyone knew it. So there's a story dating back to WWII, that when Danes would return home from abroad, border guards wanted to make sure that they were really Danes and not someone with a fake passport.

How would they be sure that someone is Danish? Simple. Just make them say *rødgrød med fløde.* Only real Danes would say it right and spies or imposters would give themselves away!

So what would your secret dessert code word be?

# Hey, We Can Fight Too!

When we hear the word gladiator, our mind's eye immediately evokes images of brave, big, scary guys who fight until the emperor shows a thumb up or a thumb down. But do we ever imagine women gladiators? We should be able to, because women gladiators really existed and they fought as bravely and as skillfully as men. Daughters of professional male gladiators often became gladiators themselves. Although they are now referred to as gladiatrix.

Ancient Rome was a patriarchal society. This means that men made all the rules and regulations, and they also believed a woman had her role which was not as important as that of men. That role was to be decent and faithful to her husband, to provide an heir for him (preferably a son), to be devoted and loving, cheerful and happy, and always look her best. Seems like the women of ancient Rome had a lot on their plate, huh?

Well, it turns out that some women weren't happy with this role. They were expected to just do what they were told and sit quietly. Some women accepted this, others could not. They wanted more control over their own life and destiny, and they found a way out... becoming gladiators (or gladiatrix).

The established patriarchy of Rome had a huge issue with this. In fact, they hated the idea of women fighting in the arena, mostly because that meant the women were refusing their traditional roles and choosing a different path, one where they weren't being controlled by men.

At first, historians believed that poor women were forced to fight because they had no other means of escaping poverty. But documents prove that there were high-born women playing the game as well, women who weren't in need of money. They fought in the arena just because they wanted to be free and to threaten the established world order.

The Roman satirist Juvenal even wrote: "What sense of shame can be found in a woman wearing a helmet, who shuns femininity and loves brute force." And Tacitus wrote: "Many ladies of distinction, however, and senators, disgraced themselves by appearing in the Amphitheatre." But gladiatrix fighting in the arena were apparently popular with the Roman crowds even if Juvenal and Tacitus didn't like it.

Whether they were loved or shunned, women gladiators are a historical reality. For many women, living in a patriarchal society under the thumb of men was unbearable. One way to fight this was to actually fight, and gain at least some control of their own fate, independent of men.

# Mummify Yourself...Alive

When you think of mummies, you probably think of Egyptian royalty, preserved and prepared for the transition into the next life. In that process, they had help. They couldn't have prepared for it themselves, for the simple fact that they were dead. But in Japan up until the 19th century, there were Buddhist monks who did exactly that. They mummified themselves!

The first question that'll pop to your mind is surely why, oh why would they do that??? Let's first see what this whole thing is about. Self-mummification in Japan is known as Sokushinbutsu, which roughly translates to becoming "a Buddha in this body."

First, let's see why anyone would want to be mummified. Many cultures hold the mummification process in high regard. Leaving a corpse behind that doesn't decay has always been a sign of something amazing.

The most famous monks who practiced Sokushinbutsu are the Japanese Shingon monks of Yamagata. What they're doing is seeking redemption for mankind. Self-mummification is a sacrificial act. They did it so that they would be granted entrance to Tusita Heaven, from where they would also be able to protect humans on Earth. The trick for Tusita Heaven is that their bodies can't decompose. It has to be bound to their spiritual selves. This is why the self-mummification process is extremely painful, long, and arduous.

What they did was mummify themselves from the inside out. The process lasts at least 3 years, and it starts off with a special diet known as *mokujikigyō*. The monk would go wandering through the nearby woods, eating only nuts, berries, tree bark, tree roots, and pine needles. This way, they would lose fat and prevent any future fat from being stored in their bodies. Basically, the body is starting to dry up from the inside as this diet lacks vital nutrients and moisture. In addition to the diet, solitary wandering adds to the spiritual journey so the monk can contemplate life, death, and everything in between.

This diet would go on for exactly 1,000 days. Once usually isn't enough, so many undergo this process several times, to make sure they'd really mummify themselves in the end. Otherwise all that effort would be for nothing, right?

The next phase is the embalming process. This was done by drinking tea made of urushi, which is the sap of the Chinese lacquer tree. It is highly toxic and the monk is drinking it so that after his death, insects won't start gnawing on his body. They're still drinking water, but very little. And they add salt to it. Meditation and contemplation continues as well.

Slowly, the monk would feel death knocking on the door. He would then place himself in a super small, tight pine box, which would then be lowered ten feet below the ground. A small bamboo rod would allow fresh air flow, and there would be a bell that the monk would ring every day as he continued to meditate in total darkness. Once the ringing stopped, the other monks would assume that he was dead. The tomb would be sealed and left undisturbed for 1,000 days. After that, they would open the lid and check the body. If it showed any signs of decay, they would bury the body because the monk did not achieve Sokushinbutsu. If it was intact, they would proceed to dress it in ceremonial robes and put it up in a special place at the temple.

Luckily, Sokushinbutsu became illegal in 1877 and rightly so. Hundreds of monks had tried to do it since the first attempt way back in 1081, but only about two dozen actually achieved it.

# The Mystery At Your Fingertips

Fingerprints are the reason why so many crimes are solved, ever since Thomas Jennings fled a murder scene back in 1910. He was clumsy, and left behind a perfect impression of his fingerprints in the wet paint on the railing. These fingerprints actually led to his conviction for murder the following year. Why? Because no two people have the same set of fingerprints. Not even identical twins. They have the same DNA, but not the same fingerprints. Huh?

So why do we even have these ridged patterns on our fingers? Is it just to identify ourselves? Two theories popped up as scientists began to study fingerprints. They either help with our grip or they improve touch perception. Most scientists preferred the first theory, that these ridges allow for a better grip by creating friction between our fingers and the surface of the object we're touching. Scientists wanted to see how this theory would hold up in a laboratory experiment. The results were astounding. The actual area of contact was reduced by the fingerprints! This means that basically, these ridges actually reduce the quality of our grip. Many scientists still believe that these ridges must somehow aid in improving our grip, perhaps when holding wet, slippery or temperature sensitive objects.

How about the other idea, that fingerprints improve touch? Our fingers contain four types of sensory receptors. Things called Pacinian corpuscles, can be found about 0.08 inches below the surface of the skin and they help with perception of fine texture. Georges Debregeas, a physicist and biologist, conducted an experiment. He created a biomimetic tactile sensor, basically a little machine resembling a human finger. This machine had sensors like Pacinian corpuscles, and he had two different versions of the device made. One with ridges, the other without.

The result? The machine with the ridges created more vibrations which would under usual circumstances be felt by the Pacinian corpuscles. In other words, it seems that we have fingerprints so that we can increase our tactile sensations. You may be asking yourself why, and that's because you don't live in the hunter/gatherer world that our ancestors lived in. For thousands and thousands of years, our hands were our crucial tools for finding food. Sometimes, just touching food made it obvious whether it was edible or not. Debregeas figured out that chimps and koalas also have fingerprints, just like us. These animals also rely on touch to find food and understand the world around them, supporting the theory that fingerprints may have evolved to help with touch sensitivity.

But...koalas aren't even closely related to us in terms of DNA. And there are at least FIVE other competing theories as to why we have fingerprints which basically means, scientists still have NO IDEA! Whatever the purpose, the whirls, loops, and arches that make up each fingerprint are unique for each person. And if you are a criminal, you have to make sure these unique fingerprints don't give you away!

# The Sandwich That Started
# A World War

Austrian Archduke Franz Ferdinand was assassinated on June 28th, 1914, by the 19-year-old Gavrilo Princip. No one could even imagine what a catastrophic chain of events this would trigger. Hint: It caused WWI. And the strangest part? All of it happened because of a sandwich.

The logic behind this theory is deliciously simple. It was a simple matter of no sandwich, no shooting. If there was no shooting, there would be no war.

You're probably all bug-eyed, wondering to yourself, how could one little sandwich cause a world war? Well, here you go. Gavrilo Princip, our assassin, stopped to have a sandwich for lunch at a delicatessen called Schiller's. And that put him in the right place, at the right time. Or the wrong place at the wrong time for the Archduke.

It probably sounds silly. A sandwich causing a war. But you see, Gavrilo needed to eat. That's not such a farfetched idea on it's own. Assassins eat too, right? And while some historians argue about whether or not he ate an actual sandwich, the point is the same. Gavrilo was at this particular deli eating lunch at this particular time.

This is crucial. Why? Because there were seven other assassins that day competing for the kill! They tried to blow up the Archduke's car with a grenade. They failed. It bounced off the car and blew up the car behind the Archduke's. That failed assassin then swallowed a poison pill and jumped in the river. The pill didn't work and the crowd pulled him out and beat him up for hurting so many people. The Archduke was fine, but a few of his soldiers were injured.

After this attack the Archduke's driver changed his planned driving route. And as sometimes happens when you change directions, the Archduke's driver got lost. Finally, someone figured out a way of getting him to the hospital, where he was supposed to meet with injured men.

The governor was in the car with the Archduke and called out to the driver that he had gone the wrong way and the driver stopped, in the worst possible place. They were just out in front of Schiller's deli, where Gavrilo Princip was chomping on his sandwich.

The Archduke and his assassin were about 10 feet away from each other. I'm guessing that Gavrilo forgot all about his sandwich at that point. And because of complete dumb luck...he had the chance to walk up and shoot the Archduke. And it was this specific event that embroiled all the major countries of the world into a giant, horrible war, affecting the lives of millions.

Not all historians believe that it was a sandwich that put these two in such close proximity. But historians do agree that it was a stroke of awful luck that put the Archduke's car right out in front of Schiller's deli where Gavrilo Princip happened to be.

The moral of the story is that even assassins eat. Perhaps sandwiches, it would seem.

# Can You Really Operate...on Yourself?

Sometimes we look at something and think to ourselves, *"You know what? I could totally make that better."* And that is how a do-it-yourself (DIY) project starts. It can be anything from painting your room yourself to making your own plane, like Frantisek Hadrava who loves planes so much that he actually made one for himself, and is actually flying it. There's a lot of stuff that falls under the category of a DIY project, as you can see. But one man took it a step further. Make that several steps further, when he performed surgery on himself!

Dr. Evan O'Neill Kane's first chance at self-surgery happened in 1919. One of his fingers had become infected and needed to be amputated. Kane was a surgeon. But most surgeons let another surgeon handle this sort of thing instead of doing it themselves. Not Dr. Kane! He went ahead and did it himself, using local anesthetics. According to him, it was a breeze.

The second time a chance presented itself was 2 years later. Only this time, it wasn't something as small and easy as a finger. Kane operated on himself and removed his own appendix! Aged 60 at the time, he did it just as easily as he had amputated his own finger. The New York Times reported his process: "Sitting on the operating table propped up by pillows and with a nurse holding his head forward that he might see, he calmly cut into his abdomen, carefully dissecting the tissues and closing the blood vessels as he worked his way in. Locating the appendix, he pulled it up, cut off and bent the stump under..."

He was familiar with the process, seeing as he'd done it over 4,000 times on other people. Mirrors were placed strategically so he could see the work area. Back in the day this operation was considered more complicated than it is now because the incision was bigger. Kane did such an amazing job that he was released the next day.

Needless to say, the operation hit the news and it brought him much media attention, mostly because it was considered the first time anyone had successfully operated on himself. It is said that Kane did this for two reasons. The first one was that he wanted to experience the procedure from the patient's point of view. The second reason was trying to prove that general anesthesia (putting the patient to sleep) wasn't always the best way to go. In operations such as this one, local anesthesia (numbing the surgical area only) would be enough without inconveniencing the patient.

Then again in 1932 when he was 70, he repaired his own hernia, also using just a local anesthetic. This time, it was made into an even bigger deal because this operation is much more complicated than removing an appendix. The press witnessed the operation at the Kane Summit Hospital, and there was also a photographer present. The operation lasted exactly 1 hour and

55 minutes. It was such a success that Kane was back to work only 36 hours later!

While his self-operations were a huge success, a disclaimer is needed. Don't try this at home!

# An Official Statement On Mermaids

We live in an amazing world. We can fly long distances, even without wings. We can stay underwater for hours, even without gills. We can prolong our lives with medicine and healthy food. But what would make this earth of ours truly magical? Finding proof of fairies, unicorns, mermaids or other mythical creatures. When Animal Planet aired a film set up like a documentary called *Mermaids: The Body Found*, and then a year later, *Mermaids: The New Evidence*, everyone went wild because these shows claimed there was proof that mermaids really exist!

Unfortunately, it wasn't true. Although the movies were seen by millions of viewers, most of them missed the disclaimer at the beginning (which was shown for less than a minute), which explained that the following program was just science-fiction based on a scientific theory. Basically they were blending fairy tales with some real life elements that suited the story. They based their "findings" on the so-called Aquatic Ape Theory, which is exactly what it sounds like. This controversial theory suggests that some of our ancestors developed in such a way that allowed them to spend more and more time underwater. They eventually substituted legs for a fish tail, all because of the necessity to find food. While most of our ancestors retreated from the water, these guys just went deeper becoming full ocean inhabitants.

The first video opened up with a supposed mermaid sighting in 2009, when someone shot a grainy cellphone video of a mermaid-like creature perched on the rocks before it quickly slithered back into the water. What followed in the first and second videos were interviews with biologists and other scientists, as well as video material taken underwater, with what seemed to be the actual footage of real live mermaids! It was amazing, and so real looking that you wouldn't doubt it for a single second. The whole world bought it, hook, line and sinker.

As you'd imagine, the internet blew up. People were ecstatic about this! It seemed that the whole world, young and old, were just waiting for definitive proof of mermaids. But as the excitement built, an official explanation needed to be released. The show's executive producer explained why they made this pretend documentary. "We wanted people to approach the story with a sense of possibility and a sense of wonder." The National Oceanic and Atmospheric Administration put out an official statement on the website (just in case): "*Mermaids: The New Evidence* is just entertainment. No evidence of aquatic humanoids has ever been found."

Still, don't let this stifle your belief. If they were real, mermaids wouldn't want to be found by humans anyway, right?

# The First Person to Ride Down Niagara Falls in a Barrel Was How Old?

If you are a daredevil who likes pushing the limits and having adventures, then you'll enjoy the story of Annie Edson Taylor. Annie was the first person to go over Niagara Falls in a barrel. She was 63 years old when she did it!

So let's talk about Niagara Falls and what makes this feat so spectacular. Niagara Falls is sometimes considered the Eighth World Wonder. This huge waterfall sits on the border between Canada and the United States and is actually a combination of three waterfalls. Horseshoe Falls is the largest and has the tallest vertical drop of 160 feet. Niagara Falls has the largest water flow rate of any waterfall in North America with an average of six million cubic feet of water going over the falls every minute. That's a lot of water!

So now that we know a little bit about the waterfall, let's get to Annie's story. Annie was born in 1838 and was one of 8 children. Her father died when she was only 12 years old, but he left enough money for the family to live comfortably. She became an honor's degree winning school teacher and married David Taylor. However, this is where her story gets a little sad. She and Taylor had a son who died during his infancy. Her

husband died shortly after that and Annie was left trying to find a job and a location that made her happy.

For years Annie tried different careers, such as music and dance instructor. She lived in different places,
Michigan, Texas, and even Mexico City. Worried about
her financial future, Annie decided that she might be
able to make a lot of money if she did something spectacular. This is what spurred her idea to ride over Niagara Falls in a barrel.

At the time, no one had gone over the falls yet and
survived. Annie had a barrel made specifically for her
trip. The barrel was oak and iron and the inside was
padded with a mattress. Two days before her planned
trip over the falls, Annie did a test run on her barrel
and sent her cat launching over the waterfall. Poor kit-
ty! Both the cat and the barrel survived, although the
cat did have a few minor cuts.

The test run gave Annie the confidence to continue and on October 24, 1901 on her 63rd birthday, Annie climbed into her barrel. She took with her a lucky
heart shaped pillow. Her friends secured the lid and
used a bicycle pump to put air into the barrel, securing
the hole with a cork. The barrel was then set adrift in
the river to allow the current to do the rest of the work.

Annie and her barrel plummeted over the falls
where rescuers were waiting at the bottom. Her river
ride and plunge took no longer than 20 minutes and
she was mostly unharmed, except for a slight gash on
her forehead. However, Annie later told reporters "If
it was with my dying breath, I would caution anyone

against attempting the feat ... I would sooner walk up to the mouth of a cannon, knowing it was going to blow me to pieces than make another trip over the Fall."

Unfortunately, Annie's Niagara Falls trip did not earn her the money and fame that she had hoped. She did have some speaking engagements, wrote a book, and posed for photographs. She died in 1921 at 82 years old and blamed her bad health and near blindness on her trip over the falls.

Since Annie's famous trip in 1901, thousands of people have intentionally or accidentally plunged down the falls, but only sixteen people have reportedly survived. Between 1850 and 2001, over 5000 bodies have been found at the foot of the falls and it is estimated that 20-30 people die here every year. The moral of the story? It's probably better to enjoy the scenery of Niagara Falls, than to try to ride down in a barrel!

# The Unhappy Drill Sergeant
# Who Became the World's
# Happiest TV Painter

Bob Ross is a name most often associated with serene paintings and a soft-spoken artist. Can you believe that this quiet painter was once a yelling drill sergeant?

Eighteen year old Bob Ross joined the United States Air Force in 1961. He made it to the ranks of Master Sergeant and was stationed in Alaska. The Master Sergeant is the head drill sergeant. And everyone knows what drill sergeants do. They yell. And they yell a LOT. They yell at you if you don't make your bed properly, if you are late to your job, if you aren't doing your best. In fact, a major part of being a drill sergeant is yelling. But Bob didn't really like to yell. He was generally a happy, soft-spoken guy and he decided that when he left the military, he was never going to yell again.

But Bob did more than just yell while he was stationed in Alaska. Being in Alaska actually impacted and changed the rest of his life. While in Alaska, Bob liked to paint to ward off the stress of being a drill sergeant. Because he didn't have a whole lot of time to dedicate to painting, he discovered a painting technique known as *alla prima* or "wet-on-wet." The artist layers wet paints, allowing a canvas to be completed in around thirty minutes. Bob perfected his technique and began painting Alaskan scenery on the back of gold mining pans and selling them to tourists. Eventually, his side business made more money than his job in the military and Bob was able to do what he'd hoped. He left his job as a drill sergeant and was able to focus on being an artist.

Bob was a skilled artist, especially at painting the beautiful scenery that had surrounded him in Alaska. Some friends encouraged him and helped finance his own television show, *The Joy of Painting*. In each thirty minute segment of the show, Bob would walk his viewers through a painting from start to finish, encouraging beginner painters. He would say, "we don't make mistakes; we just have happy accidents."

So of course, we are sure Bob would agree that it was just a happy accident that his career as an dismal drill sergeant ended so he could grow his career as a TV artist. His company, Bob Ross, Inc. ended up being worth about $15 million. Even after his death, people still know and love Bob Ross. Not only can you buy Bob Ross paint sets, you can also find Bob Ross chia pets, designed to grow like his iconic permed hair. There is a Bob Ross waffle iron, so you can have "happy little waffles." And there are even energy drinks that claim to be filled with the joy and positivity of Bob Ross!

Besides all of the paintings that Bob has done, his real gift to his viewers was his happiness, positivity, and encouragement that anyone could do anything. We need more people like Bob Ross in this world!

# The Man Sent to an Insane Asylum for Suggesting Doctors Wash Their Hands

Ignaz Philip Semmelweis, a Hungarian physician from the 19th century, is now known as "savior of mothers," for his ground-breaking work in reducing post-birth mortality rate in women. But this recognition only came after his death. During his life, he was made fun of because he urged his fellow doctors to wash their hands after each patient, especially after handling a dead body.

In 1846, Semmelweis found himself working in the "First Obstetrical Clinic" of the Vienna General Hospital. He had the usual obligations of a doctor. Examine patients, oversee the delivery of babies, and teach students. That sort of thing. While he was working there, the hospital had two maternity clinics where babies were born. They were called simply, the First and the Second Clinic. What Semmelweis noticed was that the death rate was much higher in the First Clinic.

Being a good doctor who truly wanted to help his patients, Semmelweis wondered why this was so. He ruled out overcrowding and other similar conditions. The only logical conclusion was the difference in the staff. Only medical students worked at the First Clinic, while the Second Clinic had midwives

The following year, Jakob Kolletschka, Semmelweis' friend, tragically died after he was accidentally cut with a scalpel while performing an autopsy on a dead body. Semmelweis concluded that Jakob died because he came in contact with an infection on the dead body. That must have been what happened with the mothers as well. His ground-breaking conclusion was that doctors were examining dead bodies and then without washing their hands, examining women who had just given birth, thus transferring the infection.

He immediately implemented a rule of washing hands in a solution of chlorinated lime after every autopsy. And there you have the first sanitizing gel in history. As you'd expect, the mortality rates dropped right away. Unfortunately, not many people believed Semmelweis because this theory sounded made up. It lacked scientific backing. Still, he continued washing his hands diligently. And slowly, his following grew.

But that wasn't enough. Semmelweis was believed to suffer from depression and being considered a hand-washing quack by many of his intellectual peers didn't help his mental state at all. Eventually, his own family committed him to a mental asylum when his behavior turned violent. He spent only 14 days there and then died of blood poisoning.

The modern world recognizes Semmelweis for who he was, a true genius well ahead of his time. It's sad that some of history's great geniuses had to suffer tragic lives in order for their ideas to be understood after their deaths.

# The Boy Who Quit, 3 Feet Away From Gold

Have you heard of the expression turning lemons into lemonade? It's an old saying that means you can take a bad situation and turn it around and make the best of it. And that's exactly what RU Darby did when he and his uncle lost MILLIONS of dollars on a gold mine.

RU Darby's uncle was struck with gold fever during the gold rush. He went west, claimed a piece of land and started digging. Within a few weeks he had indeed struck gold! The uncle hurried back to his family where he borrowed money from relatives to buy the equipment needed to mine the rest of the gold. Darby went back west with him and the two set to work.

A large sum of gold was mined and the uncle was beginning to be able to pay off his debts. Then, a funny thing happened. The mine dried up. Darby and his uncle continued to dig and excavate but the gold just wasn't there. Frustrated, they quit. The uncle sold the mining equipment and the claim to a man for just a few hundred dollars.

This new owner was clever and he knew that seeking some expert advice might pay off. He consulted with a mining engineer. The engineer advised him that the vein of gold had shifted because the mine was located on a fault line. Sure enough, just three feet from where Darby and his uncle had quit digging, the new owner found millions of dollars of gold.

Darby took this lesson to heart. He learned then and there that you should never be so quick to quit, and never give up.

Shortly after the mining experience, Darby learned another lesson that helped him later in life as well. He was working with his uncle on his uncle's large farm. While they worked, a young girl who was the daughter of one of the poor sharecroppers came to Darby's uncle and told him that her mama said that he owed her fifty cents.

Darby's uncle told the girl to go home. She sat quietly and didn't budge. The uncle told her a second time that he would not pay her the money and still, the small child did not leave. Finally, for the third time, Darby's uncle told the girl to get out of the barn or he would take a switch to her. The girl yelled at him, "My Mammy's gotta have that fifty cents!"

At this point Darby got nervous. His uncle had a violent temper and this young sharecropper's daughter could be in big trouble talking to him like that. But to his surprise, his uncle reached into his pocket, took out the money and handed it to the child. The child ran off and Darby learned another important lesson. Persistence pays off.

Now what do these two stories have to do with each other? Darby took these lessons that he learned as a boy and went on to become an insurance salesman.

So successful in fact, that he made *millions* of dollars selling insurance. At one time he was thought of as the most successful insurance salesman in the United States. He learned to never quit, even if things were hard. He persevered, even when people told him they weren't interested in buying his product. Hard work and perseverance made him a very successful business-man. Talk about turning lemons into lemonade!

# The $80 Champion

On a dreary night in 1956, a dirty, skinny horse was loaded onto a trailer with other horses where he was going to be driven to a slaughter house. As a horse who hadn't sold in the auction earlier that same day, this was to be his fate. Lucky for him and for his thousands of fans who came to love him, his fate changed when Harry de Leyer pulled into the parking lot.

Harry was a Dutch immigrant horse trainer in Pennsylvania. He had arrived at the auction late and almost missed his chance to purchase a new riding lesson horse for his riding program. He looked into the trailer already loaded for the slaughter house and saw a skinny grey horse with kind eyes. He made an offer of $80 and the horse was his.

Harry and his family named the horse Snowman and he became a favorite in Harry's riding lesson program. After some time a neighbor offered to buy Snowman for his daughter for $160. Harry accepted the offer and Snowman went to live on the nearby farm.

This is where things got exciting. Snowman had grown to love and trust Harry and his family so much that he didn't want to live on another farm. He would jump any fence, no matter how high and come back to Harry's stable. Snowman would jump a five foot high fence like it was nothing! Luckily, the neighbor who was tired of this escape artist's ways, sold the horse back to Harry.

Harry started showing the horse at jumping competitions where he won easily. No matter how big the jumps were, Snowman would jump them, beating the very best horses in the country. In 1958, just two years after his rescue, Snowman would be named the United States Equestrian Federation Horse of the Year. The $80 champion was beating horses worth hundreds of thousands of dollars!

The grey horse won at New York City's Madison Square Gardens Diamond Jubilee two years in a row, the first horse to ever accomplish this. He won the hearts of fans everywhere. He became known as the "Cinderella Horse" and people loved to cheer for this plain horse who was defeating the odds.

Through it all, Snowman was still a favorite in Harry's riding program and amongst his children. Harry said that sometimes Snowman would jump his pasture fence to meet the kids getting off the school bus. He loved to go swimming with the kids in the pond and was often seen with a gaggle of children sitting on his back in the water.

Snowman's fame earned him a spot on "The Tonight Show" with Johnny Carson and on the game show, "To Tell the Truth." He was written about in The New York Times and appeared twice in Life magazine. Later, there were several books written about him and even a documentary filmed.

Harry was offered a lot of money from other people who wanted to buy Snowman. He always turned them down. Harry and Snowman had a special bond. Snowman died with Harry by his side in 1974 when he was 26 years old.

# Do You Accept Checks?

On March 30, 1867, Secretary of State William Seward agreed to buy Alaska from the Russians for $7.2 million. The actual photo of the check is still circulating the web. At the time, Alaska was considered nothing but an empty wasteland and many politicians believed that it was one of the worst decisions ever. What in the world would Americans do with all that snow?

The dissatisfaction was so great that the purchase was called "Seward's Folly." Only it turned out that Seward had the last laugh. People hit both oil *and* gold in Alaska, plus thousands of tourists visit every year. It seems that Seward was a little ahead of his time and maybe a bit of a visionary.

But how did this agreement come to be? Alaska was first officially known to the world in 1741. That was when Vitus Bering discovered it and laid the Russian flag on its soil. Immediately, the local fur trade became a booming business but people were reluctant to build any settlements. The Russians didn't particularly like the unforgiving nature of Alaska. The first colonial settlements didn't appear until forty years later in 1784. And even then, those few hundred settlers weren't self-sufficient. They relied on the British, the Americans, and native tribes for many supplies.

The Russians' main concern was that Americans would take up an interest in Alaska. Then the trading of furs took a plunge. The only logical solution for the Russians was to negotiate selling Alaska to the US. Unfortunately, the Civil war broke out and the negotiations were cut off. After the Civil War, Seward was still interested in the purchase, and he entered into secret negotiations with Edouard de Stoeckl, who was the Russian diplomat in charge of relations with the United States. Finally a deal was made. The sale price would be $7.2 million.

When the news hit the streets, some people welcomed the idea but the press attacked it with gusto. They referred to Alaska with some pretty degrading nicknames. You'd see it called things like, "Russian Fairy Land" or "Johnson's Polar Bear Garden". Sounds delightful, right? The New York Tribune's editor called it "a burden... not worth taking as a gift." Ouch.

On October 18, 1867, the US flag was raised in Alaska for the first time. The event was attended by both Russian and American troops. The indigenous leaders were there too, but their vote didn't count for much at any point during the negotiations.

Seward's purchase was ridiculed for a long time but in the end, the amount of resources that the nearly 424 million acres provided the United States has been invaluable to the country.

# A Running Rebel

Rebel Hays has run in eight high school cross country races and attended the state cross country meet. That is an impressive feat for any high school student, but Rebel is only in fourth grade.

How does this fourth grader get to run out on the course with the high schoolers all year? He is a guide-runner for a visually impaired runner at West Forks High School.

Rebel has always loved to run. For five years in a row he was the winner for the local fun run. One day, while picking up his older cousin from high school cross country practice he saw Jenna and Rosie Scott running. Both girls were visually impaired. Rebel found out that the Scott's had two younger adoptive brothers who were also visually impaired and wanted to start running. Rebel knew he could help!

West Forks High School coach Tiffany Surber had seen Rebel run and knew he was up to the task. At one point, all four of the Scott children were running and Coach Surber had to reach out into the community to help find other guide runners. She was grateful for Rebel's big heart.

Rebel and Paul Scott have been running together now for three years. In 2020, they set their personal best time of 20:59 minutes, beating Paul's goal for the year of 21 minutes.

Rebel said he does get a little nervous before races, because he always wants to make sure he is able to help Paul do his best. Paul has one more year of eligibility to run for West Fork and has set a goal for 20 minutes for his next season.

So while you won't yet find Rebel's name being recorded for running in the high school meets, it's all great training and conditioning for when Rebel is running those meets as an eligible high school runner. He dreams of one day being in the Olympics and his big heart and fast legs are a great start to getting him there.

# The First Two Cars in Ohio...
# Crashed Into Each Other

The state of Ohio was the home to many of the earliest developments for automobiles. This meant that many "firsts" occurred here, including the first car crash.

In 1891, James William Lambert and his friend James Swoveland were riding in Lambert's car when they hit a tree root. Lambert lost control of the car and ended up crashing the car into a hitching post. I'll bet any horses tied to it were not amused! Luckily, no horses or humans were hurt in the world's first ever car crash. The driver, Lambert, actually went on to patent 600 different inventions, most of which pertained to the automobile. Hopefully, he was thinking about safety after his car crash experience.

Another interesting first that occurred in Ohio, was the first car crash involving two cars. This crash was in 1895. You'll be surprised to learn that at this time there were only two cars registered in the state of Ohio. And these two cars accidentally crashed into each other! This was because the roads in those days were very narrow. They definitely weren't designed for two cars to safely pass each other. But with only two cars being driven in the entire state...it's pretty weird that they would crash into each other.

The good thing that came out of these early crashes was that people and inventors had to get smart about car safety. Roads were rebuilt and designed thinking about the future with automobiles. Car designers started thinking about safety and eventually added things like seat belts and air bags.

# A 1 in 30 Million Rare Lobster Almost Eaten for Lunch

Workers at the seafood restaurant, Red Lobster, have a lot they have to keep track of. They have to remember all of their customer's orders, the recipe for those delicious biscuits, and occasionally they have to be able to determine if a lobster is an extremely rare breed. How rare you might ask? The chances of seeing a lobster of this coloring are 1 in 30 million! Those odds are actually worse than you becoming President (1 in 10 million).

The employees at a restaurant in Virginia received an order of lobsters from Maine and noticed that one of the lobsters had a unique coloring. The shell was covered with orange and black speckles. Of course, these employees see a lot of lobsters and recognized that this one had a funny coloration so they reached out to a nearby zoo. The zoo put them in touch with the Virginia Living Museum. It was determined that it was a rare calico lobster. It is the third rarest lobster in the world, after the albino and the split colored lobster. Calico lobsters rarely survive in the wild because their markings make them easy for predators to see them.

The lobster was named Freckles and was sent to live in the Virginia Living Museum, where he will wow people with his unique shell and be protected from predators.

This isn't the first time that a Red Lobster employee saved a rare lobster from being put on the dinner table. A group of employees in Ohio noticed a lobster that had a blue colored shell. Further research proved that it was a rare blue lobster. One in every 2 million lobsters has blue coloring.

The Red Lobster team named the lobster Clawde, and contacted the Akron Zoo. The zoo was definitely interested in housing this unique lobster. But after getting the lobster back to the zoo, they determined it was actually a girl lobster and renamed her Clawdia!

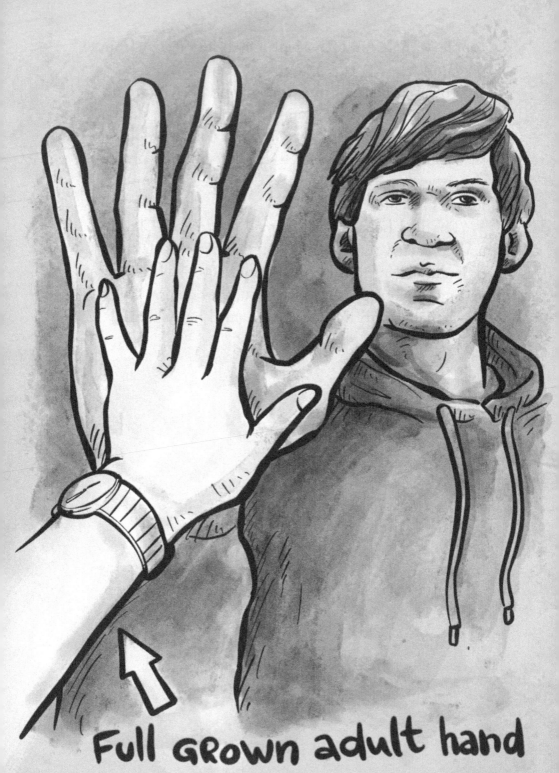

Full grown adult hand

# This Giant Might Be the World's Nicest, Most Loveable Guy

There exists in the National Basketball League, a mammoth of a man. But this isn't really that interesting all by itself. The NBA is full of giant men who are amazing athletes. But the tallest player of them all right now, actually has a heart that is bigger than he is. This man's heart and the joy that he lives life with, make him one of the most beloved players in the history of the league.

I present to you...the legend of Boban Marjanović, or Bobi, as he is affectionately known. Currently the tallest professional basketball player in the United States at 7 ft and 4 inches tall, Bobi is a mountain of a man. When he was in the 1st grade back in the small town in Serbia (Eastern Europe) where he grew up, he had already grown as tall as his adult teacher by the 1st grade!

And today he can actually dunk a basketball...without jumping. That's right. He's so big, so incredibly and delightfully huge, he can just stand there and slam a basketball through a hoop while keeping his feet on the ground. It helps that not only is he incredibly tall, but when he stretches his arms out (also known as a person's wingspan) that distance is even longer than he is tall. From fingertip to fingertip, it is 7 feet and 8 inches. Wow.

But one of the most remarkable things about Boban's body is how big his hands are. There is actually a website that only shows pictures of him holding things. And it's actually really interesting because you've probably never seen a hand THAT BIG holding a cell phone, banana, or anything. His hands make everything look like a toy. Each hand is nearly a foot long. They're massive.

But here's what everyone loves about Boban Marjanović. It's his heart and how crazy happy he is. He may be one of the happiest people on the planet. Have you ever been around someone who is really really happy? It's contagious isn't it?

But he wasn't always so happy. Boban grew up in wartime. He grew up in Boljevac, Serbia, a small town of just over 3,000 people. By the time he was 3 years old, the deadliest European war since WWII had broken out in his country. This war, the Bosnian war, followed by other conflicts, would last until he was 13. His family was poor and slept together in the same room in case they needed to find each other after a bomb exploded close by. He would listen to the sounds of the planes overhead and hope his family survived the night.

When Boban was 10, he discovered basketball. And while he was huge at that age, he didn't try dunking a basketball for another 5 years even though he could have. He says it simply did not occur to him. Nobody else was dunking, they were running around and playing the way they had to as normal sized boys. Boban thought that's how he was supposed to play too. His coach yelled at him to dunk the ball and he had to ask how. But once he did, he couldn't believe how easy that made the game!

The thing that draws people to Boban is how he wants to make everyone around him happy, even strangers. And not just people are drawn to Boban, but dogs too. He says that children and dogs are his main goal. He is happiest when surrounded by kids and animals. Somehow kids and dogs can tell that he is a wonderful person. And that makes Boban feel the best. Both kids and dogs do have great instincts when it comes to judging people.

But it's not easy being a giant. Most of us would feel awkward or shy being so different from everyone else, but not Boban. He is completely at ease being so unique. He has funny looking ears and could pay to get them changed to look like everyone else's ears. "But why?" he asks. "Never be shy, never be shy about who you are. If you're tall, you're tall. I love being big." But most of all, he loves making people happy. And that's why this man, who was once a poor boy in a small Serbian town, grew up to be one of the most loved basketball players in the world.

# The Greatest Fiasco in Swedish Naval History

The year was 1626 and Sweden had one of the most powerful navy fleets in the world. King Gustavus Adolphus wanted to cement his legacy and create a symbol of Sweden's naval dominance by building the most powerful and largest naval ship in world history. King Gustav had been in power for over 10 years and was already one of the most successful wartime rulers in Swedish history. Unfortunately, this project was doomed from the start. But it shouldn't have been.

Sweden was full of capable and competent ship builders. The King found Henrik Hybertsson, a Stockholm ship builder and hired him for the job. Master Henrik had all the resources of the kingdom at his disposal. The King allowed for a 1,000 tree forest to be cut down and used for the building of this single ship. He was determined to spare no expense at all for this project and told Hybertsson that his budget was unlimited.

The trouble soon began when the King began meddling in the project. The warship would be named the Vasa. It would have 32 cannons on its deck and be 108 feet from front to back. The lumber was cut and preparations began. But then the King decided that it should be 120 feet long even after all the lumber had been cut for a 108 foot ship. So they began building a 120 foot boat. Then the King decided that the Vasa would be 135 feet long. It's a good thing they had 1,000 trees!

King Gustav had also changed his mind about the number of cannons the boat should have on deck. Instead of one row of 32 cannons, he decided that it would be best to have two rows with a total of 36 cannons. Oh and let's add another 12 smaller cannons. And cannons took longer to make than ships. So when the Vasa was finally built, almost another full year passed as they waited on the cannons to be ready.

400 people worked day and night under the continually changing orders from the King. As they got closer and closer to being finished, they got more fun news. The King now wants 72 cannons! Soon after this news, poor Henrik Hybertsson had a heart attack and died. People said it was because of the King's constantly changing mind about what the Vasa should be.

Despite Hybertsson's death, the project went on and on and on. The money spent on it piled up and up. The King at one point decided that there should be over 700 sculptures attached to the outside of the ship. Really? Sculptors spent over 2 years creating them.

Finally, the day came for the first trip at sea for the Vasa. It was a grand celebration. There were perhaps as many as a few thousand people gathered to watch the largest ship ever built make it's very first voyage. They enjoyed a fireworks display. Important people from other countries had been invited. The King had wanted a big event. After all, quite a bit of work had gone into this ship!

Embarrassingly, the Vasa was unable to sail even one mile. As it prepared to pass by the crowds who had gathered and fire its mighty cannons as a salute, a gust of wind caught the sails. The enormous boat tipped over toward the sea with it's cannon doors open. Water rushed in. Less than 400 feet from shore, in front of all those who had gathered, the mighty and most expensive ship in Sweden's naval history...quickly sank.

King Gustav was actually in Poland at the time and when word finally reached him of the disaster, he was enraged. Of course, he blamed everyone but himself. A full investigation was launched. All survivors were questioned. The builders were interrogated. But they could find no guilty party who was responsible. And they wisely did not blame the King. They shrugged. So did the King. And so his legacy was made, but not for the reasons he had hoped.

# Get That Tower Outta Here!

What are the first things that pop to mind when you think of France? Croissants. Baguettes. Macaroons. Stinky, blue cheese with those little rotten bits inside. Yum!

But what about construction? You probably also thought of the Eiffel Tower. It seems to pierce right through the sky, demanding to be respected and adored, welcoming thousands and thousands of people every year.

Only...the French hated it at first. Like, *really* hated it. The architect who came up with the idea for this tower, Gustave Eiffel, pitched the idea to Barcelona first and they said, no way, take that ugly thing somewhere else. So Gustave did exactly that. He went to Paris and suggested they use it as the main archway for the 1889 International Exposition. The Parisians said *oui*.

The ones whose votes counted, that is. The general public hated it, just like the Spaniards did. They said it was clunky, ugly, and badly structured. One guy even went ahead and called it a metal asparagus. Eventually, they only agreed to have it because the Eiffel Tower was supposed to go down shortly after the exposition, and everyone thought, oh okay, let it hang for a while but then get rid of it.

They actually hated it so much that they offered to sell it for scrap. Only, no one wanted it even for that. But then the French Army found a way to use it. Because of its height of 984 feet, it served as a communications tower.

Even today, people either love it or hate it. But most people love it now. One thing is for sure. When people think of France, they don't only think of good pastries, baguettes and stinky cheese. The Eiffel Tower is among the top picks for sightseeing and has welcomed an estimated 250 million visitors since it was built in 1889.

I wonder if Barcelona feels silly now?

# The Giant Hole That Sucks In Helicopters

During the mid-1950's, the Soviet Union was still trying to rebuild itself after World War 2. People were looking for any way to bring wealth to the country. Geologists were searching the country looking for valuables that could be mined, especially diamonds. In eastern Siberia, three geologists found traces of kimberlite in the rocks they were testing. Kimberlite is a sign that diamonds are in the area.

With the promising possibility of diamonds, it was decided that a large mine needed to be built. The construction of the Mirny Diamond Mine was underway. It was a complicated process though, because of the location of the mine. Eastern Siberia is covered in permafrost for much of the year, making it very hard to dig. The remaining months of the year, when the frost melts, the ground is spongy and wet. This is not a good base for building. The area is also super cold during the winter, like 40 degrees below zero! Brrrr!!!! This made it nearly impossible for machinery to run properly.

Still, the Soviets persevered. They used huge jet engines to warm the ground to make it easier to dig. Thick covers were used to keep the equipment warm enough to use. Dynamite helped to blast through the permafrost. By 1960, the mine was up and running.

After all that hard work, the Soviets sure hoped the mine would be successful. Luckily, it was hugely successful. It's estimated that the mine produced 10 million carats of diamonds every year. That's a lot of bling! It produced a 342 carat lemon yellow diamond, the largest diamond that had ever been mined in the country. While the mine was operating, it produced over $13 billion in diamonds for the world.

With all of that wealth, other diamond companies began to get nervous. They were also skeptical that this relatively small mine was able to produce so many diamonds. In 1970, De Beers, the world's largest diamond supplier, asked to tour the Mirny mine to satisfy their growing curiosity about the mine's production. Permission was granted, but during the trip the actual tour of the mine was delayed so many times that the De Beers representatives only had 20 minutes inside the actual mine.

After that brief tour, the mine remained a carefully guarded mystery that continued to churn out billions of dollars worth of diamonds.

In 2004, the mine was closed. Officials said that flooding had occurred and that the mine had been dug too deep to safely mine any more diamonds.

This means that the very small town of Mirny, now features a giant hole in the earth that is 1722 feet deep and 3900 feet wide. It is one of the biggest holes in the world. It's so big in fact, that the airspace above the giant hole is restricted. This means that planes and helicopters can't fly directly over it.

The reason?

They could be sucked into the hole!

The deeper into the earth that is mined, the warmer the air in the hole becomes. This air, when mixed with the bitter cold air from outside the mine, creates a windshear. This would mean that with the rapid air temperature change, a helicopter would lose altitude incredibly fast. The pilot would likely not have time to react before the aircraft crashed. Several incidents of helicopters crashing into the mysterious pit have been reported locally, but nothing can be confirmed. Russia likes to hold on to its secrets.

# Radioactive Spider Bites

In the marvelous world of Marvel heroes, it seems that all of them are somehow too special to be even a little human. All are either born into superpowers or somehow come into contact with them and retain them. It makes the characters pretty unrelatable. Well, this is exactly what Stan Lee wanted to change. So he, along with the help of a few other people, created Spider-Man.

In a time when everyone, including Lee's boss, expected superheroes to be adults, it was hard even suggesting a teenage superhero like Spider-Man. Lee's boss said it would never work. First because of the teenager aspect, and then because no one liked spiders.

Still, Lee pushed on. While he was working on the Hulk and the Fantastic Four, he was looking for this simpler character, a sort of everyman. One day he saw a fly on the wall, and he thought how awesome it would be for a man to stick to a wall like an insect. So he tried some names. Mosquito Man. Insect Man. Pretty terrible, right? Lee seemed to think so as well.

Then it hit him. Spider-Man. Strange and mysterious. Dramatic and a little bit off-putting. Lo and behold, a legend was born.

From then on, Spider-Man took the world by storm. Lee always said he liked Spider-Man because he was the most human superhero. He's not perfect. He doesn't do exactly the right thing at exactly the right time. On the contrary, he makes mistakes all the time. He's got so many problems he has no idea where to turn. He keeps hitting a stone wall in almost every episode. He does things wrong, but that's okay because he always tries to fix things. This is what makes him so relatable. Almost like it could be any one of us, hiding underneath that red and blue mask.

In the end, despite what most people told him, Lee went ahead and put his previously rejected story in the final issue of a book. It eventually led to an entire Spider-Verse being created, with not only comics appearing, but also movies, TV shows, incredibly popular video games, etc.

So, next time you enjoy yet another episode of our friendly neighborhood Spider-Man, remember to thank Stan Lee, Steve Ditko and Jack Kirby for sticking to their guns and pushing on, even when others told them what they were doing would be a total fiasco. It turned out that people would indeed love the idea of a teenager being bitten by a radioactive spider.

# You WON'T Pop Your Eye Out?

Sometimes the moment just doesn't seem right for a sneeze (or a burp or a fart...but that's another story), and you think the best thing would be to just hold it in. What harm can it do, right? Wrong. It can do a lot of harm.

Holding in a sneeze can cause some serious pain. It can even break a rib! You don't believe me? Just ask Phil Hughes. What happened to our buddy Phil is the stuff that jokes are made of. He figured he'd just hold in a sneeze, and go about his day. Only that's not exactly what happened. Phil Hughes, a pitcher for the New York Yankees, held in a super giant sneeze and ended up with a stress fracture on one of his ribs. It took him five months to recover from it. Crazy, but true.

Let's see what happens when we sneeze. When you sneeze, you expel air at about 100 miles per hour. That's fast. So if you try to keep the force of this punch inside, it can cause some serious issues. This is especially true if you have an underlying medical condition like osteoporosis (a disease which makes your bones weaker), or cancer.

I'm sure you've all seen those people who try to suppress a sneeze by pinching their nose and closing their mouth. Seems bullet proof, right? Well, not exactly. That air still needs to get out somehow, and the force of that blow is such that it can actually rupture your eardrums or do serious damage to your inner ear.

There's this story about a woman from Massachusetts, who after trying to suppress a violent sneeze, ended up in a neck brace. Or the one about Sammy Sosa, a Chicago Cubs slugger, who sneezed twice and sprained a ligament in his lower back. Seems this sneezing business is no joke!

But at least your eyes can't pop out if you try to suppress it. Why? For the simple reason that you can't keep them open. A very small percentage of people can, but the rest of us are closed-eye sneezers. Still, even if you did manage to keep your eyes open somehow during a sneeze, they wouldn't pop out because your eye sockets are made of bone. They don't have muscles to eject them. And your eyes aren't connected to your nasal passages.

So yes, your insides can get totally busted if you try to suppress a sneeze, but at least your eyes won't pop out. A silver lining, right?

# Weird Things About Abraham Lincoln's Assassination...

Abraham Lincoln wasn't the first (or the last) president to be assassinated. However, there are some aspects of his death that still amaze and even baffle historians. There are still so many questions. For example, where was Lincoln's bodyguard? Why wasn't General Ulysses S. Grant with him, as planned? Who besides Lincoln, might also have been a target? And how did the assassin manage to escape a theatre full of people?

Real life writes the best stories. And quite often, some loose ends remain untied.

Let's start digging for answers. So where was General Grant? Did you know he was supposed to be there? A few days after General Lee's surrender, Grant accepted Lincoln's invitation to attend the play "Our American Cousin" at Ford's Theatre with him and his wife. But rather interestingly, Grant's wife wasn't very fond of Lincoln's wife, so she made Grant come up with an excuse not to attend the play. Mary Todd Lincoln could be pretty tough on people and had recently lashed out at the general's wife.

And where was Lincoln's bodyguard, the man who failed at the only task he was supposed to do, keeping Lincoln safe and sound? According to some sources, it's believed that the bodyguard, a man by the name of John Parker, was there for the play but decided to have a quick drink at the saloon next door during the intermission. Good grief! He ended up staying there much longer than he intended to. He was supposed to be at the door to Lincoln's booth, doing his job. But he wasn't, and it was his disappearance that made all the difference.

Strangely enough, that saloon was the same place where John Wilkes Booth went to steady his nerves right before the actual assassination. So the assassin may have sat right next to the bodyguard before the killing. And Booth didn't originally plan on killing Lincoln, just kidnapping him. But after General Lee surrendered, Booth decided mere kidnapping wouldn't be enough and he'd need to go all the way.

Which is exactly what he did. He killed Lincoln, and actually managed to escape Ford's Theatre alive despite breaking his leg in the escape. He was in hiding for 12 days, aided by Confederate sympathizers, who provided him and one of his helpers, David Herold, with supplies and medical help. Eventually, they were found on a Virginia farm where Booth was fatally shot.

Booth's father, Junius Brutus Booth, 30 years earlier had threatened to kill another president, Andrew Jackson. Junius Brutus was the name of Julius Caesar's assassin. It seems this whole family was obsessed with assassins. John Wilkes Booth had portrayed Brutus on stage only months before killing Lincoln.

# The Doctor Who Ruled A Country...
# Only To Lose His Head

A monarchy works based on the principle of the heir. Sons inherit their father's title, and become kings. Then, their sons do the same and so on. In the case of a daughter, she marries and then her husband becomes the ruler of whatever country we're talking about or she rules herself. It's pretty basic stuff. So how did a simple doctor rise to power and actually control all of Denmark?

Johan Friedrich, Greve Struensee came from a religious family, with a theologian father. He studied medicine at the University of Halle, and was a very ambitious student. He was elegant, charming and highly intelligent, all of which helped him land the prestigious job of the king's physician. This happened in April 1768, and already by May, Struensee was bestowed with the honorary title of State Councilor. How's that for charming?

This was just the beginning of his slow but steady rise to power. He got the king and queen to be on friendly terms again. The queen, Caroline Matilda didn't like him at first, but he paid attention to her and that was enough for the lonely queen to take a liking to him. The king was mentally ill, and paid absolutely no attention to his young and quite lovely queen, so it was easy for Struensee to swoop in.

He continued to be very hands on with everything in the castle. He oversaw the upbringing of the prince, spent a lot of time with the queen and advised the king, who had grown to trust him completely. In May 1770, he became the royal adviser, then a few months later he appointed himself the privy counselor, which is when his real time of power began.

The king's mental condition continued to degrade, and Struensee just kept controlling politics in the country. At first he wanted to remain in the shadows and just use the king as a puppet to do his bidding. But he was impatient and greedy. So he abolished the council of state and appointed himself the only person who could present reports to the king. You see where he was going with this, right? The king had no idea what was going on, and Struensee made all the decisions he wanted.

All department heads were dismissed, too. The cabinet, with Struensee as the main guy, was the only authority in the entire country. He had absolute control of what was going on, and no one could touch him. And he was rather busy during those thirteen months. He issued about three orders a day, which included stuff like abolition of torture, abolition of noble privileges, abolition of some holidays, abolition of the Royal Court's aristocracy, criminalization and punishment of bribery, and so much more. A lot of those orders are quite good, right?

Initially, people liked him, especially the middle classes. But they still didn't like how he just pushed the king aside, and some even believed Struensee had been lying to everyone about the king being insane. But even worse, he fell in love with the queen.

In all this, Struensee had a close ally, Enevold Brandt, a Danish courtier. Brandt got into an argument with the king (because the king wasn't really *that* mad and sensed that they were using him), and Brandt ended up slapping the king. That was a big no no.

A palace coup took place in 1772 (it's when the government is stripped of its power aggressively, usually by some new dictator), and Struensee, Brandt and the queen were arrested. Struensee was accused of "usurping the royal authority in contravention of the Royal Law." Basically, he was charged with scamming the Royal Court. He claimed he was innocent but no one believed him. He and his accomplices were sentenced to lose their right hands, be beheaded and then have their bodies pulled apart. Yikes. Quite a punishment.

Even after Struensee's death, the king still thought he was a good guy. From the looks of it, the king *really* may have been stark raving mad after all.

# The Oldest Hotel in the World

The Nishiyama Onsen Keiunkan spa hotel holds a prestigious Guinness World Record. You might be tempted to think the record is for the best hotel in the world, or maybe the comfiest beds or something like that. No. It is the proud bearer of the Guinness World Record for the oldest hotel in the world.

When I say old, I mean really old. The name of the hotel comes from the time when it was first opened, which was in the 2nd year of Japan's Keiun period. When was that? Care to take a guess? It was 704. And no, that number isn't missing a 1 in front of it.

Since the first moment they opened their doors to the public, the hotel has remained in the same family, which is a staggering 52 generations! Of course, the hotel has changed quite a bit since then with the addition of modern era equipment and other amenities. But all of the water used in the hotel is still from the nearby hot springs. In fact, the water from the springs is so hot that the hotel doesn't even need to have a water heater.

The calm and relaxing surroundings and ambiance haven't been sacrificed for the addition of modern amenities. There are several hot springs to choose from, all famous for their relaxing and healing properties. Four outdoor options and two indoor options all feature mineral water sourced from the earth said to help relieve muscle and stomach pain as well as improve skin tone.

It's no wonder then that the hotel has accommodated some pretty famous guests, like movie stars, singers, and other celebrities. But it has also hosted plenty of historical figures. For example, Takeda Shingen was a famous samurai warlord who ruled Yamanashi back in the 16th century and he chose to spend some time there for rest and relaxation.

In 2005, the hotel underwent some major renovations which mainly focused on adding a private flowing hot spring to every single room in the hotel. As you can imagine, this was a rather pricey endeavor, and unfortunately it hasn't been as lucrative as management had hoped it would be. Cheaper hotels in the area have brought a decline in the number of annual bookings to the historic hotel.

Still, the hotel's owner has stated his wishes to "Continue operating a single ryokan and preserving its traditions, while working hard to improve its hot spring, cuisine, and service." Hopefully, with its excellent service, ambiance, and history, this hotel gem will continue to operate for another 1300 years.

# The Guy Who Had
# Hiccups...for 68 Years

Hiccups. We've all had them. They're quite annoying, aren't they? Those involuntary contractions of the diaphragm that cause our bodies to react. Fortunately, they usually only last a few minutes and you just have to wait them out. Problem solved.

But what happens when that problem isn't so easily solved? When you wait and wait and wait. And then you wait some more. And suddenly you realize you've been hiccuping for 68 years?

Sounds horrifying, right? And almost unbelievable. That's also what Charles Osborne thought about it. He figured he'd just wait it out. It eventually took him 68 years of waiting for his hiccups to finally stop. True story. Just ask the Guiness Book of Records, because that is the longest bout of hiccups ever recorded.

So how did it all start? One afternoon in 1922, Charles had some farm work to do. He was weighing a hog for slaughter. He said that he was hanging a 350 pound hog, and when he tried to pick it up, he slipped and fell down. This was the beginning of his endless hiccups.

The frequency of his hiccups was about 40 times per minute. Ouch. Then mercifully, that number went down to 20 hiccups per minute. He even managed to suppress the noise just by learning to breathe slowly and deeply between the hiccups, a method he was taught at the Mayo Clinic.

What about his life? I think that hiccuping like that for years on end, would be enough to drive anyone crazy. But not Charles. Despite all this, he actually managed to lead a normal life. He married twice. He had eight kids. The only change to his everyday routine caused by hiccups was the fact that he had to process his food in a blender when he got older, because the hiccups were making it harder for food to reach his stomach.

Then he woke up one morning, and the hiccups stopped. Just like that. Absolutely mind-blowing, right? Too bad that it happened only a year before Charles died, so most of his life was spent hiccuping. 68 years of hiccups and 29 years being hiccup-free.

And the cause? Dr. Terence Anthoney, who treated Charles at a later point in his life, believed he knew the answer to this puzzling question. When Charles fell down trying to pick up that hog in 1922, he apparently busted a blood vessel in his brain which damaged the exact part that was responsible for hiccup control.

This seems spot on, especially if you take into account a few other cases of year long hiccups. For example, Christopher Sands, a musician and a vocalist, hiccuped for 3 years when doctors found a tumor in his brain stem. When they removed it, he was back to normal.

So you shouldn't have to worry about this the next time you have the hiccups. Just relax and breathe slowly or try holding your breath. But people probably told Charles that too, the poor guy.

# Shakespeare's Curse...Couldn't Save His Head

On the grave of the most famous author of all time, you will find a strange inscription. It might be that it was his final piece of writing. It is widely believed that Shakespeare himself wrote it.

*"Good friend for Jesus sake forbeare, To dig the dust enclosed here. Blessed be the man that spares these stones, And cursed be he that moves my bones."*

If you're like me you can hear a very spooky voice reading those words. And if you know what's good for you, it's best to try and avoid curses of the dead. But not everyone is so respectful of the wishes of the deceased. Because apparently, not even that threatening curse on the great playwright's grave...could save his head.

Okay, that's pretty wild. First, let's explore how Shakespeare died. It was over 400 years ago in 1616. His death is a mystery as well. He was just 52 when he died, which was young for a wealthy person. Theories swirl about what happened to him.

Some say it was Syphilis, others suggest he contracted Typhoid fever which was common in those days. And still others push another popular theory of...murder! Shakespeare had actually cut his son-in-law out of his will before he died which might have

SEYMOUR Del.          MASON Sculp

given the young man motive. Thus, poisoning is one theory of how Shakespeare could have died.

But back to his grave. Is his skull really missing? And if so, who in the world took it?

Argosy Magazine published a controversial story all the way back in 1879 that was widely discarded as fiction. It claimed that in 1794, a man named Frank Chambers was paid to steal Shakespeare's skull. He and a grave robber gang then carried out the grisly crime. This caused quite a stir at the time. But experts countered that it couldn't be true. This was because the details from the story said Shakespeare was buried in a shallow grave without a coffin which didn't seem right.

Then in 2016, archaeologists used radar scans to investigate what was buried underneath Shakespeare's grave. What they found was shocking.

The body was indeed...missing it's head!

They also discovered that he was only buried 3 feet deep and there was no coffin. The details from the account from 1879 suddenly seemed rather accurate.

There are only guesses as to where Shakespeare's skull might have ended up. Sometimes loved ones dug up skulls and buried them in other locations or in other family member's graves. Seems weird today, doesn't it? And did the curse get revenge on whomever may have disturbed Shakespeare's bones? This is yet another mystery that continues to swirl around the great writer's death and what exactly happened to him afterward. The hunt for Shakespeare's head continues...

# YOUR REVIEW

What if I told you that just one minute out of your life could bring joy and jubilation to everyone working at a kids book company?

What am I yapping about? I'm talking about leaving this book a review.

I promise you, we take them **VERY seriously**. Don't believe me?

Each time right after someone just like you leaves this book a review, a little siren goes off right here in our office. And when it does we all pump our fists with pure happiness.

A disco ball pops out of the ceiling, flashing lights come on...it's party time!

Roger, our marketing guy, always and I mean always, starts flossing like a crazy person and keeps it up for awhile. He's pretty good at it. (It's a silly dance he does, not cleaning his teeth)

Sarah, our office manager, runs outside and gives everyone up and down the street high fives. She's always out of breath when she comes back but it's worth it!

Our editors work up in the loft and when they hear the review siren, they all jump into the swirly slide and ride down into a giant pit of marshmallows where they roll around and make marshmallow angels. (It's a little weird, but tons of fun)

So reviews are a pretty big deal for us.

It means a lot and helps others just like you who also might enjoy this book, find it too.

**You're the best!**

From all of us goofballs at Big Dreams Kids Books